THE TELLING OF
ANNA ELIZABETH

The beginning is the end.
That which is found is lost.

by Elizabeth M. Steele

Charleston, SC
www.PalmettoPublishing.com

The Telling of Anna Elizabeth
Copyright © 2021 by Elizabeth M. Steele

Paperback ISBN: 978-1-63837-496-1

Acknowledgements

As time has come and gone, it has left many changes all over the world. I have tried to touch on some of the more important ones throughout my writing. They have impacted all of our families; some good and some bad.

Many of the childhood experiences portrayed in my book reflect on my own childhood.

I wish to thank my husband, extraordinaire, Dr. Robert Steele, for believing and encouraging me to write. Thanks go to my daughter, Alesia, my sister, Elva and to my sister Dolly for giving me the inspiration to write. I also want to thank my many friends and family for having the desire to want to read what I write.

CHAPTER 1

I woke up this morning with the sun streaming through my bed-room window. Was this different from any other morning? I had a feeling that somehow was different, maybe a nostalgic feeling. I had nothing planned for this day; there was no hurry to get up, and I could just lie here and soak up the casualness of the morning. As I looked out the window, I could tell that it was going to be a nice day—the sun is up, birds are chirping, and a dog is barking in the distance. A soft wind was blowing the rose of Sharon against the window. I tried to dose back, but the thoughts in my head were dancing all around. So I reflected on my life as clearly as it was just yesterday. Suddenly it dawned on me that today was my birthday and that's what was different today. I am eighty-seven today, but there is no one around to help me celebrate. I am alone, and there is no one to call me, wish me a happy birthday, and even to know that today is my birthday. As I reflect back on the life I have lived—the many days and nights, sunrises, sunsets, storms, joys, tears, disappointments, loves—it seems like a long dream. Many changes have taken place in my lifetime in this old world, almost too numerous to mention. There has been a lot of suffer-ing in many lives through war, famine, diseases, and poverty, but through all that, progress has been made in economics, the scientific medical field and everyday way of life.

They say every family has secrets, and mine definitely had them. As the years have gone by and people have passed, there's no need to keep them secret anymore, or, for the most part, to mention them at all, because there is no one to tell them to, but one must remain secret, at least till my life ends. Before, when the family members were still living, they would have had consequences to deal with if their secrets were told. Then my, my sister's, and especially our father's lives would have been different; bless his soul. It was better just to let things be.

The First World War started in 1914 when Archduke Franz Ferdinand, heir to the Austro-Hungarian Empire, and his wife, Countess Sophie, were assassinated by a Serbian nationalist. Bosnia and Herzegovina had been annexed by the Austro-Hungarian Empire in 1908. The Serbs did not like it and rebelled against Austro-Herzegovina rule. It ended in 1918, leaving much devastation, but that was the beginning decade of growth. My father fought in that war as a proud soldier, but he returned wounded and remained crippled for the rest of his life.

—✠—

It was back in the era of the roaring 20s and 30s that my family and I had moved to the city from the country side. Lots of people were moving to the country after the war ended in 1918, and my father and mother had employment in the city. I was a young girl of nineteen, living in London, England. My life seemed to feel magical, coming of age; I had become an adult. My hair stood out above the crowd as it was thick, long, and burnished red. My figure was that of a ballerina—tall and lean. I wanted to bob my hair, because that was the raging style. Most of my friends were married by now, but my father wanted me to go to the University of London for education. They admitted students regardless of religion or sex, and I was one of the lucky ones. London had suffered so much from the war that many people were living in poverty, but the economics were picking up. England had great opportunities to study for young girls. I had no idea what I wanted to accomplish in my life at this young age, but I knew that I liked to help sick people, and I had seen so much destruction and death from the war and plagues that it had broken my heart.

Everything around me was changing, and businesses were booming. It was a new age of revival. Women were throwing those hot, tight-fitting corsets away and straight, loose-fitting dresses were coming in style. We were tired of wearing dresses of yards and yards of lace and satin. While they were beautiful and sexy, they were also uncomfortable and expensive to make. We wanted to be free and comfortable. Not to mention, commodities of material were hard to come by because of the shortages that the war had imposed. It was a different world—exciting and fascinating to my young body and mind. They were the years when women's suffrage finally won, because we wanted to have the same rights as men.

As I reflect on that time, I wish I could go back—back to those years of being young and experiencing that magical emergent of my life. Every now and then, my mind flashes back, just for a few seconds, and I feel young again. Oh! What a wonderful feeling it is! Then the realization hits me that I'm old. Gone are the fresh, smooth skin and bouncy steps. *So where am I now?* I ask myself. Am I in a new dimension in time, just waiting for the next phase? What is the next phase? I try not to think of it. What will I leave behind? Will I just be a fading thought for anyone—gone, and would that be it?

I stopped at a coffee shop on the bustling street that was full of shoppers and people going about their work week. More women were working now, and some of the shops were owned and ran by women. They worked mostly in the manufacturing factories, and they had finally won the right to vote. The coffee shop was full of people, and not a table was available. I started to leave when a man who was sitting alone invited me to sit at his table. I was reluctant at first, but I was famished.

"My name is Johann. May I ask yours?" he asked as he introduced himself.

"My name is Anna Elizabeth," I answered.

"And are you enjoying the beautiful weather?" he asked.

"Yes, it's a very nice day," I replied.

"I think it's a marvelous day, too," he said. "May I order something for you?"

"Yes, tea please, iced India frappe and ginger sandwiches."

I tried not to stare at him. His coal-black hair as well as his beard and mustache were carefully groomed and clean-cut, and his fingernails were meticulously cleaned and manicured. His stature was medium, and his hands and complexion were smooth and manly. He was dressed in a starched white shirt and a fashionable tie. I guessed him to be about the age of 25. There was something about him that drew me to him, a feeling that I had not experienced before and that sent wave links from my toes to the top of my head.

"Are you a student?" he asked.

Yes, in the fall at the university," I said. "It will be my first year, and I'm excited about it, yet a little apprehensive." The masculine scent of his cologne filled my nostrils.

"No need to be, you look like a bright young girl. You'll do fine," he said.

We exchanged the usual chit chat about family and friends. His voice thrilled me as I listened intently. I could feel his eyes penetrating my very being, and I felt so shy that I found it hard to look into them. My hands were shaking as I was glancing across the table at this handsome man. I wanted to learn more about him.

"Oh look, here is your order, enjoy it and have a nice day," he said as he put on his hat, and I watched as he walked out of the coffee shop. His stride was that of a proud man with a sure step. Maybe he was an athlete. I watched him till he was completely out of sight. *Would I ever see him again?* I wondered about all the things that a young girl's mind like mine wanted to know.

I wandered around the streets, peering into shops. Clothes meant a lot to me back then. I marveled at the new styles. I normally shopped with my best friend, Amelia, with whom I had been friends since we were two years old. I can't remember why we weren't together that day, but I knew that I felt alive and energetic to be alone. I had a sense of freedom, and I was beginning to enjoy it. You might say that I had led a sheltered life, for my parents had kept me close. I had never dated anyone, and we kids always went everywhere together.

I passed a saloon where a new music was playing. I think they called it jazz. It sounded very strange to my young ears. People were dancing in a new dance style called the Charleston. I could feel the rhythm in my very soul wanting to come out. My better judgment told me that I should not go in. What was happening to me? I had different feelings and thoughts, and I wanted to dance and release all the inhibitions and energy I had—to cut loose and be free. I wanted to drink and be happy like those people who were dancing and not worry about going home to my parents. Women were smoking, and I wanted to try that, too. They looked very fashionable with those long, rhinestone-studded cigarette holders sparkling in the shadows. Some were making smoke rings as I watched them swirling around in the air from the outside of the window.

I opened the heavy glass door and went in. There were colored lights strewn from the ceiling. A fog of cigarette smoke floated heavily through the air, and a band of horned instruments was playing a peppy tune. The smell of cooking odors mixed with the smell of tobacco and alcohol and women and men's perfume filled the air. A young woman was busy carrying a round tray with four or five glasses of drinks. Another scantily clad woman with a tray of various brand cigarettes was visiting each table. There were three or four couples on the dance floor, dancing that new dance style. I sat at a table for two and was mesmerized as I watched them. *Such rhythm!* I thought. It looked like so much fun. I could feel it permeating in my body, and I couldn't keep my feet still. *If I had a dance partner, I might try to learn.* I thought.

As the music ended, my eyes wandered around the room, and, in a corner, I saw a familiar figure. It was Johann, and my heart skipped a beat, for I thought I would never see him again. Was this a coincidence or was this meant to have happened? I envisioned his arms around me pulling me close to him and his warm, passionate lips on mine. My vision was lost as I watched him rise to pull a chair for a young woman as she approached his table. She was dressed in a red, short, fringed dress, and her coal-black hair was bobbed in the new style. Why should I care? I had just met this guy. But my heart was broken, and I slowly left with tears in my eyes. *Silly girl,* I told myself, *forget about him, for he's probably a womanizer and breaks hearts of all women.*

Oh, as I ponder upon my life, my mind gets entangled with all the emotions I experienced. It is like a computer with mixed-up files—some are corrupt, some have been deleted, and some I can't find. What should I put in this folder and which ones should I put in another. I wonder what I should name them.

CHAPTER 2

Mary was my only sister, and she was two years younger than me. She had light-blonde hair like the sun and blue eyes like the sea. I was always protective of her, because she was my little sister. She had a kind heart, especially for animals. She passed away ten years ago. We were definitely destined to be together for all time and eternity. I still see her tender, bright eyes as I hear the wind caress the leaves on the trees. I hear her faint voice whispering to me, and, at times, I think I smell her perfume and see her over my shoulder, but when I turn around, there is nothing there. Mary was as wonderful a sister as I could have ever hoped for, and I miss her so much.

We loved to play in the forest, where the birds and the wild flowers grew, and we especially loved the wild violets and little white flowers. In the spring, all the wild fruit blossoms tantalized our noses with their sweet aroma. The forest was down from the cotton and corn fields and the old barn above the house where we lived and milked Old Lady and Jean, the cows. Only our mother could milk Old Lady, and if anyone else tried, she would kick the bucket, and they would lose all the milk they had milked. I don't know why that suddenly changed one day when she quit letting Mum milk her, too. It was about the time when we thought Mum was acting funny, but we didn't know why. We rode Jean like a horse, well almost; she didn't like us straddled across her back at all. The crickets sang their melodies, as if to welcome us to their theater. After a soft rain, little green frogs would croak in their baritone and old bull frogs in their deep bass chant. Together they sounded as if they were having choir practice readying for their royal king and queens' arrival. We would often make our play-house by gathering up pine straw to make our beds and walls near the little babbling brook that trickled a soft melodic sound that was our music to play by. We would pick the plump and delicious fresh berries that the forest yielded up and the red, wild plums that were so sweet and tantalizing to our lips. We learned to not eat the persimmons till they were soft and completely reddish orange, or we would have a puckered up mouth. The creek where we would have to cross to gather up the cows for milking was our swimming hole. We loved to wade and feel our bare feet on the rocky bottom of the clear, cool water of the deeper spots. How we loved to wander everywhere and follow the cows' path as we had to find and round them up for milking. The thick muscadine vines were so towering that we would swing like Tarzan on them to cross the creek yelling his call. One Sunday afternoon, after church, a friend came home with me to spend the afternoon. She was a little chunky and weighed more than me. Unfortunately as she was swinging across the creek the vine broke and she fell in. I felt so bad especially because the water was so cold. I didn't know at that time how much I would miss the enchanting forest and everything the country provided for us, and I didn't want to grow up and ever leave.

The sea was close by, and my father often took us out on the sailboat to fish when we moved to the city of London. We had learned to fish and swim in the creek, but the sea was different. The salt-water fish were so different from the fresh water catfish, bream, and perch we often caught in the creek. It was always exciting to feel the sea wind on our faces and watch the mesmer-izing sunsets as they settled down over the clear, turquoise, and sparkling water. Learning to sail the boat took some practice for us. Learning the wind directions and tying down the sails strength-ened our small girl muscles, and learning all about the different ropes was quite a challenge. There were lots to know about the rigging, the winch, the tiller, the backstay, and much more. Our father made sure that we were informed and knew how to sail in case of an emergency. Our bodies were as brown as the dark sand on the beach and our hair was bleached light by the towering sun. Each summer, we could almost feel our bodies growing, and we couldn't wait to become an adult in one sense, but still didn't want this magical time of our lives to ever end.

—⚌—

My dad was a loving man but very strict when it came to Mary and me. His name was Colin Blankley, and he ran a small haberdasher for Mr. Dyland after the war. Many of the shops now were being converted into chain stores which made for competition for Mr. Dyland, but he wasn't too worried as he had loyal customers who enjoyed his always up-to-date styles and wide variety. My mother's name was Olivia, and she made hatbands for men's and ladies' hats and stylish headbands for women. I loved to sort the beautiful feathers and brightly colored ribbons for her, and hats were of a new, hot style. I think they made everyone feel fashionable and refined. With this change, everyone felt full of life and new energy, and everybody liked to have them. It was part of the new, booming economy, political, social change, and high fashion. Everybody needed a change after the devastating war. There were many styles, and the most popular styles were the fedora, the boater, the bowler, the berets, and the cloche.

Andy Parsons worked in the store as a sales attendant. He was young and a smart dresser, but he was also stiff and lacking the social skills I thought he should have. He had a boyish look about him with a sparse beard and mustache, and when he smiled, it seemed to be a forced one. I tried to joke with him from time to time, but he never quite got any of them, and I wondered if it was my jokes; no it was him. Maybe he was an unhappy guy. I never saw him with a female friend. For all that, I don't think he ever had any friends, but he did his job and would always stay after hours to put up late-arriving merchandise and, for that, father and Mr. Dylan were thankful.

—∿—

Going to the university was difficult and fun at the same time, if you can imagine that. My father stressed to me that I was to go there for an education, and not for a social life. He was very adamant about what he thought my life should be. Many of my classmates thought different, for they took this as an opportunity to exercise their freedom from parental guidelines. They liked to drink, party, and have sex. I had never engaged in sex, but I wondered what it would be like. My mother threatened me with the fear of God if I ever got pregnant out of wedlock. Some girls did get pregnant, and they were disgraced and sent to a home for unwed mothers. Some of the babies were adopted out and some went to the orphanage. Believe it or not, some of the babies were passed on as their mother's sister or brother and was claimed by their grandmother as her child. In that day in time, an unwed mother was definitely a disgrace. Actually I knew very little about sex and the human body. Sure I can't lie, I have had sexual longings. Sex in our family was a taboo to talk about. My mother did not even tell me about a woman's menstrual cycle. When mine started, I thought I was bleeding to death. Even married pregnant women mostly stayed at home and tried to hide their pregnancy. Most women had their babies at home with a midwife, and either a number of babies died or the mother died.

CHAPTER 3

Jacob McKenny was a handsome chum with black hair. He was tall, and had the bluest eyes I had ever seen and a quick smile for everyone. One day, he was walking down the side walk at the college and because we were both loaded down with books, I stumbled and we accidently collided into each other.

"I'm so sorry, let me help you," he said.

"Oh, it's my fault, I wasn't watching where I was going," I replied.

We both looked at each other in the eyes as if we were hypnotized.

"I'm Jacob McKenny, I've seen you around campus," he said.

"Yes, I've seen you, too. I'm Anna Elizabeth Blankley," I responded.

We walked for a bit, then sat down on a bench, and talked for what seemed like hours. I had completed my second year at the university and he had completed his third year. We began dating, and it was getting harder and harder to control our attraction for one another. The longing in the pit of my stomach was a constant companion when I got near him or even had thoughts of him, but I couldn't even compare them to the memory of Johann. I never forgot that day two years ago when Johann and I met in the coffee shop and later in the saloon. I even went to the perfumery shop and tried to find his scent of cologne. I purchased a bottle of Chanel #5 for me and said to myself that I must be a strange girl. When I was out and about, I was always hoping that I might see him. I thought I saw him a couple of times, but when I got closer, it was someone else. I was still a virgin, and I wanted Johann to be my first. Unfortunately, I hadn't seen Johann again and didn't know if I would ever see him again.

Jacob and I dated a few times and the longing need a woman feels could no longer be denied. I had never seen a naked man and especially someone who was sexually aroused. I had always wondered about the sexual act. Now I knew as I could feel his hardness as his warm lips found mine and his body was pressed against mine. I could feel his hot breath on my neck as he un-zipped his fly and began to unbutton my top and raise my skirt. His hands felt my soft breasts as I yielded to his demands. The wave of sensations was nothing but heaven as he thrust in and out, each one more sensuous than the one before until the ultimate of all hits—that mountainous plateau, and we both were spent to total pleasure and contentment. Although sex with Jacob was great, there was something missing in our relationship, and we began to grow apart. It didn't help either when I saw him kissing another girl in the shadows on a park bench. I was upset, but I thought better to find out now than later. My feelings for him were already on a downhill run. I began to feel a sense of relief as the days passed, and I dove harder into my studies.

—⚹—

The country was still feeling the effects of the war. A number of the returning soldiers were shell-shocked and found it hard to get back to normal life and employment much less to maintain any kind of social or family life. Many soldiers came back with mental problems. They were afflicted with posttraumatic stress, severe anxiety, headaches, and depression, and their nightmares were so violent that many were admitted to mental facilities, just to name a few. Many were found wandering around the countryside like hobos and going from farms to farms looking for food in the fields or hoping that some charitable families would give them some hot food. They would steal clothing from clothes lines. Everyone kept their doors locked. The military knew very little about psychology and how to deal with such soldiers. More stress had to be put on the training and care of mental patients. London began to realize this and began building more facilities for their care.

Aside from the psychology of the soldiers, many came back wounded, which made an impact on the medical fields. Doctors scrambled to take care of them. They had to have much more training and research for the different conditions they now had so far no or so little of.

Despite mental conditions, medical workers were already dealing with a pandemic of diseases. Polio, diphtheria, measles, scarlet fever, and syphilis, among others, were prevalent. Scientists were stressed to develop vaccines for these deadly diseases. A childhood friend of mine was stricken with polio at six years old. I had spent many nights at his family's home. His sister was one of my best friends and his father was our church minister. Everyone in the community was upset. It was on a Saturday night that we got word and that he was rushed to the hospital. His legs would no longer work; they were limp, and he had to wear metal braces and crutches. He hated those braces. He preferred to just use the crutches and just sling his limp legs to walk. Unfortunately, he wore those braces for the rest of his life.

—⟋⟋⟍—

My father, having served in the war, always told us stories, but he did not tell the horrifying facts that I knew he had been faced with. He did experience a broken leg and arm that left him with a limp for the rest of his life. I can see him now, walking down on a summer day on that old dirt road with one crutch and Mary and I running as fast as we could to greet him. I was eight years old and Mary was six when he came back. Although I was just four when he left, I had kept his picture by my bed and remembered him holding my hand on our way to church. Mary only had an image of him with stories Mum would tell us about him. We would run through the fields of wild flowers, wondering what it would be like to have a dad and to sit upon his lap and wrap our arms around him! What a wonderful experience it was for us to have our dad back. We hadn't seen him since he enlisted in the military at the beginning of the war. From time to time, we would get a short letter from him, but we checked the mail box religiously everyday—hoping for just a note. It's so sad that he never knew the family secret or maybe it was best that he didn't. I was happy that he was home again and didn't seem to suffer too much from the war except a few nightmares and that eternal limp. He and Mum seemed to have a few problems getting used to each other again after being apart for so long, but they made it a point to get familiarized with each other again, and it finally worked. Dad thought that Mum had changed somewhat from the woman he thought he had left behind. Dad was a good father and wanted us to have a happy childhood. Mum to us had changed, too, but we thought it was because she was getting used to Dad being back. Anyway she was a good mama and took good care of us, and we loved her.

Since Dad could no longer walk behind old Jack and a plough on our fifty-acre farm, he decided to sell the farm and move into the city of London. Businesses were flourishing and needed proprietors. He had known Mr. Dylan years ago and had always stopped by to visit him when we went to shop in the city. Since Dad needed a job, he had asked Mr. Dyland about one. An agreement was made between them, and Mum was offered a job, too. The farm was put up for sale. Mary and I knew that we would also miss our woodland playhouse; the sweet fruit that the forest rendered; and the cotton-tail rabbits, the deer fawns, squirrels, and all the other residents of the green forest. Yes, and we would also miss the creek that we called Blankley Creek. How could we do without gathering the beautiful wildflowers for Mum?

The farm was sold within three months, and we packed up and moved to an apartment building. I was eleven years old now and life for us had changed. There was no more bouncing out in the early morning to feed the farm animals, milk the cows, or gather the garden. We even missed hearing that old Red Island rooster that used to flog me crow. And we missed the fresh eggs. We could hear the bustling street outside our bedroom and people with those new cars that delighted in blowing their horns. Motors were roaring, and it was definitely the roaring 20s. I think they did this for attention, just to say, "Look, I have something new." Social status seemed to be important to some. Many people were employed at the Oxgate Lane Crinklewood Auto factory. The streets of London were filled with bicycles, horses, buggies, and the new cars. Mud and urine littered the streets and created a real stench as well as covering them with layers of dung. The factories left a cloud of lingering soot that seemed to cover the streets and storefronts with a gray coat.

Mr. Dylan had a shiny, black Bentley, and he kept it so clean that you could see your face in it. Sometimes he would take us for a ride back out to our farm. It had little pull-down table trays on the back of the front seats, so if you went on a long trip, you could take sandwiches, and you would have a table to eat on. We thought we were real special to get to ride in such a fancy car.

Of course we had to change schools. Daddy made it plain and simple that we had to get a good education. He would say, "It is hard enough for a woman in this day and time, and she needs an education, and no telling what they will be faced with." Before the 20s, education for women didn't seem that important and only nineteen percent had a higher education. Women were used in the war to make bandages and munitions. They cared for their families and worked in the fields. Now with the impact of the economy and the stretch of women's rights movement, an education was more important. They were tired of men speaking for them and having all the rights that they didn't have. Even the ones that were lucky enough to attend college were snubbed and ridiculed by their male counterparts. Jobs, other than domestic jobs, were harder for women to find, and if they were lucky enough to find them, they were paid way less than their male coworkers who did the same work.

It was heartbreaking to leave our little one-room school house and Miss Molly, our teacher. The thought that we would never see our best friends with whom we had played all our lives was also heartbreaking. We wondered, "What was it going to be like going to school in the big city with city kids?"

—

Mary blossomed physically earlier than I did. Her eyes were so blue that you would get lost in them. She had a figure of a model and a soft, gentle voice. Her hair was long, thick, and blonde, and she mostly wore it down in soft ringlets. She was not as assertive as I was, and she was kind of shy. Being so attractive, she was inundated with suitors, and I was always watching after her to protect her, as she was my little sister. She met this special guy, Harvey Johnson, whom our family approved. He worked in the auto factory. He was soft spoken like her and seemed to love her very much. They dated throughout her college years and got married upon graduation. She opened her own dress shop and did very well, and I was lucky enough to get my clothes at a discount. Of course, when I was not busy, I enjoyed helping her with her accounts and went to the wholesale markets with her.

Mary, my beloved sister, began to change somewhat as time went by. She began to have dreams every night, and they were so real to her that they began to get entangled in her everyday life and began to become such an obsession to her that she wanted to sleep too much. She took sleeping pills so she would sleep more, and we suggested to her to see a psychiatrist. She hired someone to manage her shop, because she had to come home to sleep so she could dream. Being as close as we were, she began to confide in me and told me about these dreams that she believed were real. She was dreaming about this wonderful man, tall, handsome, gentle, and kind, and they were madly in love with each other. They made mad but tender love, unlike with her husband. The sex was so fulfilling. They went places with each other and had fun—all of the things a blissful couple in love would do. He was wealthy, and they lived in a mansion on the outskirts of London. She dreamed that the garden was overflowing with beautiful flowers that sent their sweet aromas through the air and everything else was as fine as money could buy.

Harvey was dumfounded. We were all astounded over this. We had never even heard of this ever happening to anyone before. How could this happen? She no longer played her wifely role and soon stopped going to her shop. The whole family thought that she must get some help. Harvey could not compete with this perfect man, this make-believe person who dominated his wife's life and was destroying his. Why was this happening? How could this happen? Mary was finally convinced to seek treatment, and within the next year, she began to get better. All these dreams were an accumulation of what all girls dream of, and it was like a fairytale with her prince charming. She still dreamed of her lover, but in the past tense. She dreamed that he was killed in an automobile accident. This was a suggestion while she was under hypnosis. It worked, but now she was grieving. This was a good thing, because now she began to turn to her husband for comfort and began to have an interest in her shop again, and finally, she was back with full force in the running of it.

CHAPTER 4

Maggie Smith turned and walked away, and she didn't look back. She had been in a mental institute since she was twelve years old. Before that, she had been in an orphanage since two months old. The mental hospital had so many patients after the war that they tried to release as many as they could. Some of the less-violent ones were released to their relatives or just released to the streets to fend for themselves. All she could find out about herself was that she was placed at someone's door in a basket with a note saying, "Please take care of my baby." She was fourteen now—mature for her age and street smart. The streets were full of children, dirty, ragged, and sick from malnutrition. They were almost as filthy as the London streets full of dung. They would beg hoping for a pound or two to buy food, and they made their lean-to shelters close to restaurants, so they could pilfer through their garbage can for leftovers after they closed. They would steal from the outside produce vendors. Gangs of children of all ages would stick together to feel like they were family. They would make lean-to shelters out of cardboard boxes found in dumpsters and sleep together at night to stay warm. She had learned to fight to keep men off her. Maggie had had a troubled life. At the orphanage, she was always in trouble and bitter about everything and everybody. She was very intelligent and knew how to blame her bad behavior on someone else. At first, it worked, but she then started being violent, and everyone was afraid of her. One day, she broke a girls arm and laughed about it. At times, she was uncontrollable. Angry and wondering how could a mother not want her child! She felt unwanted and unloved. She had no one.

One day when Maggie was roaming in the streets, she saw a young girl about her age that looked like her. She must be her sister, she thought. The young girl had two children with her. Oh, how she wished she had a family like that with such beautiful children and a home to live in. Would she ever have one? She looked at herself, her hair unkempt, her clothes dirty, her shoes with holes in the soles, and no socks. Her body was frail and weak. She followed her for a couple of streets till she left in a car. Her hopes were that she would see her again soon.

—⚬⚬⚬—

College was still a challenge for me, but I found it amazingly interesting. So many people needed help both medically and mentally. I was finding it hard to decide which field I would be going into, maybe "mental" to help the war veterans. A new instructor arrived that morning and was being introduced to all the students, Mister Johann Wilson. I was so shocked at seeing him again, my heart fluttered and I felt faint. Could this be happening? I prayed to God that it was. Many of my nights had been filled with dreams of him and fantasies that were beyond my control.

We talked of our meeting a while ago in the coffee shop and how delighted we both were to have met again. I could not hide my feelings for him and I thought he recognized how I felt. He was my instructor and I was his student and there was that barrier there that we didn't need to cross. Months passed by and I began to notice little extra glances from him in my direction and I knew he was getting interested in me. My heart was beginning to explode with the possibility that he would ask me for a date. My dreams were to come true.

—⚬⚬⚬—

The room smelled of bamboo and cedar. There was a soft rain outside the window and candle lights glimmered softly in the distance. The Victrola was playing "Always" written by Irvin Berlin. I turned my head to meet his kiss. I had longed for this to happen with Johann and wondered what it would be like to have someone you deeply loved to make love to you. The intense longing was between my legs, wanting to be touched. He began to undress me and unbuttoned my blouse slowly and tenderly. Every nerve in my body was tingling. Then he lifted my skirt off, and then my underwear. He rubbed his hands over my body, seeking every inch. He threw his shirt off as he unzipped his fly and stood there, his eyes feasted on my body as his arms wrapped around me. Our bodies entwined together, and his tender and warm lips met mine with a deep but loving urgency. Now I understood how it felt to really love the man of my dreams, and Johann was everything I thought he would be.

—⟋⟍—

I began to help out in Mr. Dyland's shop with the accounts, and it helped pay for my education. I enjoyed seeing and talking with the customers. London was on fire, economically, especially now after the war was over. Women and men were anxious to try on the new styles of hats and clothing. Mum worked diligently to make the different hatbands. Headbands for women were popular, too. Many were made of feathers, beads, and sequins. Furs were coming in style, fur collars and stoles. Mink coats were a symbol of class and wealth. Women were smoking and using the long cigarette holders and elbow length gloves. Smoking was becoming a symbol of class, too. A lot of fabric, all of new designs, fringe for the flapper and chemise dresses, sequins, and beads were being stocked. I was artistically talented and helped with the advertisement, too. I wrote the store specials on the store front windows with liquid shoe polish and drew the different items on sale.

I felt different now that I had fully become a woman. Experiencing sex with Johann was life changing for me. I knew I loved him desperately and couldn't do without him, and I hoped he loved me just as much, and that we would continue to see each other. I felt a tinge of guilt because of having relations out of wedlock. I was scared that I might get pregnant. Birth control wasn't considered good at this day in time, but our feelings for each other were so strong that we couldn't restrain ourselves.

We both worked and studied so hard that it took up much of our time. Johann was working on the team to develop new vaccines for the dreaded diseases that the country was plagued with. So many were dying, and it was so heartbreaking pandemic. Many of our neighbors succumbed to influenza and pneumonia. Malaria and scarlet fever were just some of the diseases of that period of the nineteen thirties. The x-ray was invented to help identify brain injuries and bone breaks during that time and it was a godsend to the medical field.

There wasn't much time for a social life back then, but we enjoyed our close-knit family. Like most families, we tried to stay at home and make our own entertainment rather than go out among the general public and get exposed to everything. Working among people was enough exposure. We tried to stay at a distance and wear a mask at all times. We used a lot of alcohol to help keep everything disinfected and wore rubber gloves.

—m—

Andy Parsons worked very hard in Mr. Dyland's shop. He was a shy man but always courteous to everyone. He lived in a small apartment above the store. There's nothing much I can say about him except someone told me one day. "He's smarter than you, because he knows what you know and what he knows, but you just know what you know." I was beginning to find that out. I didn't think he was ever interested in a lady friend. He wasn't an unattractive man. It was just his body language that said, "State your business, thanks and goodbye." One day, a short woman with her hair rolled up in a bun and less-than-stylish dress entered the store. I couldn't help but notice that she was openly flirting with him. I watched his reaction. She kept getting closer to him as she was asking about a certain kind of hat, and I was astounded to notice that he was not backing away. He showed her all the different styles and she purchased one and left. The next week, she came back and asked for Andy. I said, "Well okay, first name basis, what's going on with the boy?" She said that she wanted to look at the hats again and that she saw one last week and would like to try it on again. The store was nearly empty of customers. He took her back to the fitting rooms and I thought that she was trying all of them on. I don't know what went on back there, but when they came back, both were blushing. She didn't buy that hat or anything else.

Although Andy was a strange little feller, he took care of the ordering in his department very well and always seemed to know what the current styles and colors were. He was always on time and always followed the same routine. His posture was straight up with his nose in the air. He was meticulously dressed with a bow tie to match every outfit, and his shoes always shined so much that you could have used them as a mirror.

All in all, Andy Parsons and Dad always got along together, even though they weren't pals, they made great business associates. Mum liked him, too. He always called her Miss Mum, and he called me Annie and Mary, May.

CHAPTER 5

Dad was born on January 23, 1893 into a large family. He had six brothers and six sisters. Born right in the middle, he did not feel much of anything, that is, not much love or attention from his father. His mother died in childbirth along with her child. Dad found his father at their grave one day trying to dig them up. It took months before the family was able to smile about anything. Life seemed like a dark hole where everyone in it could not find a way out. All the chores were carried on like clockwork, just like before, but with such sadness and not much conversation as before. The family was poor as most of the folks in the surrounding country side. Trying to survive was the main concern of his father and his large family. Everyone was taught to work, and, to work hard, and since they were left without a mother, the older siblings had to care for the younger ones. Household duties also had to be shared by all. The fields where they lived were always being prepared for the upcoming planting or harvest. They relied on the fields, forest, and streams for food. Almost all the farmers borrowed against their crops in order to buy seed and fertilizer at the co-op stores. When the crops came in, they would pay it back, but they were at the mercy of the weather. When there was a drought, many weren't able to pay back and lost their farms. Also, they raised hogs, cattle, and chickens with a few ducks and horses thrown in. The English winters were hard, especially on the farm animals, and shelter had to be provided.

As with all growing families, there were more problems. Dad's oldest brother drowned while trying to rescue a calf. It had gotten away while being tied with a grass rope and ran into a swift flooding creek after a hard rain. Somehow the calf fell on him, the rope caught him under water, and he couldn't get free. More sorrow was added to the family, but they had to struggle on and try to find some kind of joy and purpose in life. The local priest and parishioners gave much comfort to them as they prayed together for strength to cope with this hard life.

Dad and his siblings did manage to get an education in the little one-room school house several miles from their house. They had to walk to school, but they didn't mind. Getting up early and doing chores and doing chores again when they returned was expected of them. All this, and finally having to do homework by the light of the burning fireplace, pretty much tuckered them out. On cold winter nights, the old irons that their mother had ironed their clothes with were wrapped in rags and placed in front of the fireplace to get hot. They were put at the foot of the cold bed, and they put their feet against them to keep them warm at least till they got the bed warm. Quilts were made out of the scrapes left when their mothers and grandmothers sewed their clothing. Most of the quilts were called utility quilts that were not fancy and were used to keep everyone warm on those cold nights. When they had some extra time, the women, especially in the wintertime when there was no field work, pieced the fancy patterns like the wedding ring. Most of these were given as wedding gifts. Most of the women embroidered and crocheted scarves for their dressers and knitted warm caps and sweaters for the winter.

Miss Hurst was their teacher. She was fiery, strict, and made sure that everyone paid attention to her. No one slept in her class. They wouldn't even think of it. She knew that many had to rise early and feed and milk the cows, and so she made extra time for them to do their homework in class. She made learning exciting and devised many ways to keep them alert. Oh sure some were rowdy at recess, especially the boys, but she would come with her hickory stick, and no one wanted to rile her.

—◊◊◊—

London was beginning to experience a population surge. Beginning in the 1900's the population was roughly five million and rising to over seven million by 1911. With the rumors of war, many couples married and many babies were in the making. Unfortunately many were born, never to see their fathers.

I finished my medical degree in 1936. Johann was still studying his vaccines. He and his colleagues developed several vaccines that proved solid for some of the diseases that plagued the nation, but we did take time for ourselves. The following summer of 1937, we decided to marry. This was such a thrilling time for me, as I was so in love with him. Every time I saw him coming through the door, it felt like I was putting a decadent piece of chocolate in my mouth. He was such a wonderful man, very intelligent, kind, and tender, and I couldn't imagine my life without him. The very idea of marriage and sharing life with him as his wife was ultimate happiness. In our third year of marriage, I discovered that I was pregnant. We couldn't have been happier to have an addition of a baby conceived in love to our world. A bouncing baby boy was born as healthy as he could be, and we thanked God for all our blessings in life. Manning was such a sweet baby, and he grew so fast. He learned to read by three and loved to write his name on everything. His vocabulary was outstanding for his age. One day, Johann emptied the hot coals out of the fireplace to clean it. He forgot to lock the kitchen door. Manning had an old straw hat that he carried around a lot, and he went out in the backyard and had it over his face, and he stumbled right into the hot coals.

It's so hard for me to think of it now of our poor child being burned so badly. We took him to the hospital where he stayed for three weeks, but infection had started in, and he succumbed to death. The infection was too much, and penicillin had not been discovered then. Sir Alexander Fleming accidently discovered it in 1928, but he was not able to produce it for the public at the time, and it was not highly publicized. We were so devastated. Johann blamed himself. I tried so hard to comfort him by telling him that it was just an accident. He became depressed so bad that he had to start psychiatric treatments. I thought they seemed to be working, but Manning's birthday was a trigger for him, and I found him hung by his belt the next morning.

They say that each day is a gift that God has given to us and that we should untie the ribbons. I tried to practice this. It was such a horrifying time of my life after losing a child and husband. I stayed as busy as I could by taking care of people. Holding back tears and memories proved to be the hardest thing I had ever done, but I was adamant that I would not let depression sneak in. I prayed each time I felt that lost feeling, slowly trying to take control. Nights were the crying time when all was quiet and I was alone in the bed that I had shared with Johann with so much love and happiness. I decided to redecorate the whole house. I got rid of everything that we had shared. I gave all of Manning's things, his baby bed, clothes, and toys to a young unwed mother. I could get rid of all their material things, but I couldn't wipe away the awful loss and hurt that was unending. Fortunately I had God, family, and friends to turn to. I began pouring myself in my work at the hospital. I forced myself to be joyful to everyone and especially warm and tender to those who had or would likely lose a loved one.

They say time heals all things. It is true to some extent. I found myself getting more excited about life, and the days were not so exhausting. I found new energy and satisfaction in my work as each day dawned. My patients seemed to give me hope and were just as therapeutic to me as I thought I was to them. A friend of mine gave me a cat. I had always loved animals, but had never had a cat. I named her Princess. She had soft, long hair and glowing green eyes. She immediately became a lap cat, a friend, and a companion. I seemed to know what she was saying with each meow and she became a great comfort to me. With each breaking day, she was my alarm clock. I didn't know cats had a sense of time. She greeted me each evening when I arrived home with a special meow. I'm afraid I spoiled her with those chicken treats.

Mary was still seeing the psychologist and was doing well. She was too close kin for me to be her doctor, but I kept close tabs on her. The shop was doing well, too. Jane Williams worked for her, and she was the one to whom I gave Manning's things. She was very thankful, and I was glad that she could use them for her baby. She was from a family of ten and had to work to help support them. The baby's father was a soldier killed in the war. She was an attractive girl and many of the male customers always asked for her. She did her job well. Mary was even thinking about making her manager. I was always, when I had free time, up for babysitting. Her son was such a good baby and he had coal-black curly hair and the sweetest smile. I'm afraid that I became too attached to him, but I didn't realize that I had. I knew that he filled some of my lonely hours with absolute joy. I think Jane figured this out and she began to keep him with her family members. It broke my heart that I got to see him only occasionally at the shop, but I understood. What can I say about my life at this time? I had the sweet memories of Johann and Manning, and I had many pictures of them together. Johann was a wonderful father and I was thankful to God that I had them at least for a while. They taught me many things about being a wife and mother. These things, I thought, I would never experience again. My father, mother, and Mary were my lifelines, and I clung to them for I fought each day to find a little joy in it. I kept finding peace and self-satisfaction in my patients. There's a euphoric feeling when you have helped someone overcome a physical or mental condition. Knowing you have been a factor in improving someone's life is very gratifying, and I was thankful to God for the ability to have the knowledge to allow me to do this.

Being in the medical field, practicing psychology was hard to understand when it happened to you or a loved one. I found it easy to help most others with their problems, but forgiving Johann for leaving me weighed heavily on my mind. I know that he felt responsible for Manning's death, he just could not bear his feelings of guilt any longer, and his grief was too strong. Nevertheless I had to find some peace and joy in this life and some way to forgive him.

CHAPTER 6

Maggie Smith, street-smart Maggie Smith, laid her head down on the burlap pillow on a bed of old newspapers. Above her was a make-shift tarp roof. There was a soft rain beating softly as she pulled an old blanket snugly around her neck. She was not sleepy, just hungry. The restaurant had closed early and hadn't emptied their garbage, so she would have to wait till the morning breakfast crew came in to shift through the cans for food. She did not like to do this in the daylight, because people would see her. She had fought another girl the day before for a banana, but by the time she got it, it was squished badly. The park was her only place to get water at a fountain, and she strolled through it daily to stay off the crowded streets. She was cold from the tiny leaking hole in the tarp, but she would have to wait till the morning sun to dry out.

As the morning dawned and the sun began to rise, Maggie felt a new beginning. She had concocted a plan to get her out of this. She was older now and knew that she wouldn't last much longer on the streets. She had found a place where she could slip in and wash up. Not many of the streeters knew about it, but clothes were a problem. Maybe she would get enough in her tin can to buy some from the Salvation Army thrift store or get some from the shelter, and she could pick up some makeup that she had never used. She could steal some from a store, but when she went into one, she was always followed and watched. She didn't blame them, for it was because of the way she looked and smelled. Things had to change, for life on the streets was getting worse day by day as more people were faced with evictions and more were let out of the orphanages as they aged.

The fact that she did not know about her family was always nagging Maggie. They had to have lived somewhere close by unless they moved away. Was her mother or father still living? Did she have any brothers or sisters? Were they put in orphans homes, too? Answers to these questions were always on her mind. When she was younger, she was a habitual offender for fights with other streeters. However, as she was getting older, she wasn't getting into as much trouble. Kept in juvie, she at least got a cot to sleep on and three squares. Lots of bad things she did, she had been able to get away with. She believed that she had killed two others. One was trying to rape her. She always carried a knife in her bosom, and she just stabbed him and ran. She didn't stand around to see if he lived or died. She just knew that where she stabbed him, there was a lot of blood. Another was a woman who was trying to steal her food that a generous person had given her. She didn't wait around then either. Maybe she had stabbed another one, yes, she had. That one died for sure. She couldn't remember why she did that one though. It didn't even bother her. Having dealt with this kind of life from the very beginning was the very best rationalization she could give for her demeanor. It was called *"survival,"* under the worst of circumstances.

When she could sleep, she would sometimes dream of having a mother, father, and a nice home as a child and growing up in that home, going to dances and theaters, and eating at fine restaurants. Sometimes she dreamed of having fine, clean clothes that smelled good and a nice, soft bed to sleep in, whereas other times she would dream of having a family of her own, her own house, and a kitchen in which she could cook delicious meals. She dreamed of having sweet children of her own and a loving husband that adored her. Those were just dreams. When she woke up, she realized that she was on the street, hiding behind an alley, with an old make-shift blind made with an old tarp that she found in the garbage dumpster. Her stomach was empty, and she tried to cry those tears that she couldn't cry anymore.

—⟋⟍—

Mr. Dyland began to rely more and more on Dad and Andy for running his store. He had no children to help him in his later years. His wife had passed ten years ago. It was all he could do to drive that shiny black Bentley to the store. One day, he came and asked Dad to lock the doors for a meeting with him and Andy. He had some papers in his hand. Dad thought that Mr. Dyland had sold the store to someone and that he was going to lose his job. It was just the opposite; it was his will. He thought they should know what to expect at his death. The doctor had given him less than six months to live. Dad and Andy didn't know what to say. They just knew that they would miss such a great, kind businessperson who had grown to be a part of the family. He had stated in his will that he was leaving Dad the store and Andy was to receive ten percent of the revenue produced. He was giving the Bentley and his holdings in the bank to Mum and his house and property to me. It's where I live now. He left Mary the contents of his safe deposit box, which contained numerous stocks, bonds, and momentous. I never asked her the value of all this, but I knew that it was a considerable amount. He had also paid off the mortgage on her house and shop. Sad to say, but he passed two weeks later.

The passing of another loved one brought images of my lost family. Again, it was hard to fight back the depression and to become a dweller in that dark hole. But again, I had to promise myself that I was going to be strong and I prayed harder than ever for God to give me the strength to conquer the darkness that was trying to creep in. It had been twelve years since I lost Johann, but it was just as fresh on my mind as if it was just yesterday.

Mr. Dyland's house and three thousand acres of land was finally probated. I took comfort in knowing that he loved me enough that he wanted me to have it and to live in it. I put my house for sale and began packing boxes in anticipation of moving. Mr. Dyland's house is a large Greek Revival house built in 1756 with three stories. I knew it was a large house for just me to live in, but I didn't care. It has been very well maintained and has the most exquisite of furnishings. I couldn't bear the thought of it sitting empty. I had the means to redecorate it, but it was perfect just the way it was. I only wanted to put a few of my special touches to it.

The house is called Rosehaven, probably because the English flower is a rose and because of the many rose gardens all around the grounds. I had never seen so many varieties of roses, and their fragrance was intoxicating. There are six pillows of solid yellow pine that supports the roof and front porch and painted a brilliant white. It is my understanding that termites did not like yellow pine. The outside siding consists of hand-poured red bricks. The two cellar walls consist of the same type of bricks. The roof is covered in slate. Inside, there is a large, wide hallway with sitting areas on each side and large painted portraits of the forefathers of my family. Huge gold-gilded mirrors make the hallway look even larger and more elegant. Two large, crystal chandeliers hang towering; cascading their brilliance over the already-stunning entrance. The end of the hallway leads up to two winding stairways on each side, leading up to the second floor. One side of the hallway is a large ballroom that occupies almost the entire west wing. The arched ceiling is twenty-five feet high. The walls are of black cypress panels. Some of the walls are painted with murals of the Victorian era with ladies of bouffant hairdos with long, clustered curls and laced satin dresses. The men also have the white clustered curls, top coats, and just below knees tight pants and buckled shoes. The scenes are of couples dancing around in gardens. Some are in quite compromising sexual positions.

Although the outside is beautifully landscaped, the farm needed life. I loved farm animals and wanted to stock the farm with cows, horses, chickens, and pigs. It reminded me of the farm we had while growing up. I didn't only get a farm but also beautiful sunrises and sunsets, cotton-tail rabbits, deer, all the wild animals, birds, and butterflies. I love to see the wild geese and the herons that build their nests high in the pine trees on the island of the lake. The many creeks and ponds are stocked with all kinds of fish, and I love watching them swirl and jump up in the crystal-clear water. The wild flowers with their colors of the rainbow sway their pretty heads in the wind throughout the pastures and hillsides. God's paint palette, I called it.

—∽—

I look all around and wonder and marvel at where I am now. How everything changes so easily and so often. Nothing ever stays the same. It is as if I have just blinked my eyelids and I'm transformed into another being and transported to another place here on this earth. I am just somewhere in time and that somewhere is another place that is unfamiliar to me. My surroundings are different and my body is different. I look down at my arms and hands, wrinkled with red and brown spots. I look at my figure, gone is my slim waistline; I look like my Mum. I now think of Mum, what she was like over the years, and how we grew up to become the kind of women we were. Oh, what memories I have.

—∽—

Mum was strange at times, and we all tried to understand her quirks. Dad had a way with calming her when she went on her journey to wherever she went. She also seemed to have a memory problem, and she had to have regular psychiatric care. Nevertheless she was a good mother to us and enjoyed her job at the shop. Whenever she wasn't working at Mr. Dylands, she was at Mary's shop. There was never a mention of her dad or mother or anything about them except that they had died when she was small. She had a sister who had died in infancy, stillborn, she thought. I couldn't ever remember any grandmas or grandpas, for they all had died of one thing or another. Dad said that his mother had been a midwife, as most babies were born at home. He and Mum married in their middle teens as most married early back then.

The all-time peak of London's population in its urban areas was reached to about 8.6 million in 1939. Most of the growth was outside of the County of London. The early twentieth century had seen the fastest growth than any other century had ever seen before. The growth was mostly with the expansion into the neighboring counties of Kent, Essex, Surrey, Hertfordshire, and Middlesex. The expansions also included the cleanup of the slum areas and the stench of the streets from the dung produced by the horse-drawn carriages.

There were so many economic developments in my lifetime not just in London but also in the world. There was also a major downfall—the stock-market crash of 1929. Some lost so much money that they committed suicide by jumping out of buildings. London managed to fare the worst effects of the Great Depression because of their industries of automobiles, chemicals, and electrical goods. Other parts of the country did not fare so well.

Since I had moved to my farm, I cut down my days of work at the hospital. I didn't work much anymore at the shop unless they had something special going on. Mum had to quit her job, too. She wasn't very healthy, physically or mentally. She did some strange things, and Dad relied more and more on Andy so he could take care of her.

I posted a farm work notice on the shop window because I knew that eventually I would need someone to help on the farm. All of my instincts told me that I shouldn't have gotten the few animals to have to take care of, but what's a farm without animals?

I loved the two baby calves that would rub their heads against me, just wanting a pat and rub on their heads. The rabbit's fur was so soft and cuddly. Chickens wanted to be loved, too. They can be walking in front of you and just lie down, wanting to be picked up. They would follow me everywhere I went and the two milk cows always thought that I had some sweet feed for them. I didn't try to ride any of them though like I did when we were children on Dad's farm.

Two weeks later, I interviewed several prospects. One I thought was too old to handle the heavy bales of hay and be able to do the carpenter work that needed to be done. The second one was younger, about forty, maybe. He was experienced and had worked on farms before. His face and arms were tanned a deep bronze, and he wore a short-sleeved shirt that strained his arms at the sleeves. His hair was black with a touch of gray at his temples. His shoulders were wide and solid, and his frame was lean and tall. He took off his Stetson hat as he approached me. "Howdy, Ma'am'," he said, "I'm Brett Larson about the farm job; it's so nice to meet you." We sat down and chatted about his experience and what his chores and responsibilities would be. I can't lie, he reminded me of the time when I first met Johann. I felt like a school girl again. What was wrong with me? I didn't ask him if he was married or not, but I had to keep a professional relationship, and I meant that's all it would be.

Brett came the next day and I had prepared the tack room in the barn to be his room. It was a nice room equipped with a stove that he could cook on and a nice, comfortable cot. Unfortunately, we had no bathrooms yet, but I was told some were beginning to get installed. The Johnny house was close by and there was a hand pump on the well for water. He had his own tools to work with. Mr. Dyland had left his tools too, but now he, hopefully, had everything he needed.

The two cows and calves were getting out of the pasture, and fence fixing was first on the list. I would soon see just how handy this handy man was. The barn needed painting and the stalls cleaned, and I had one cow who was about to drop her calf. I always got so excited every time a new calf was born on my dad's farm when I was growing up. Their fresh new faces and their pink noses stole my heart. Trying not to get too attached to any of my animals was definitely a hard thing to do. I knew that one day when they got older, they would have to go to the sale barn. The farm was going to have to pay its expenses if I was going to live here.

It's not easy to live alone and not having any children when you have to rely on your family that is your sister and parents, both busy with their own lives and running their business takes most of their time. As for me, I still had my patients to care for and being in the kind of medical field I was in kept me on call at any time. I've been called to someone contemplating suicide. Sometimes others were trying to control their furious rage toward another person. Sometimes it was sadness over a heartbreak or loss of a loved one. Some were just out of control. They couldn't face life or understand how to be alive in this old world. Some had panic attacks, and they simply needed a little time for it to pass. Life definitely has its challenges, and it was a challenge for me to try to make a difference. Being still young and healthy enough at this time, I dove headlong into every ambitious challenge thrown at me. Being able to help in some way gave me a great feeling of being needed.

I had to decide if I wanted to plough and plant the fields. Mr. Dyland had just let them grow hay that he had cut and baled for sale. At one time, crops covered the whole fields. Everything from corn to soybeans and some crops of vegetables and melons were grown.

We didn't know much about Mr. Dyland. We just knew that he was a good man. His wife passed away some years ago because of the flu. I think they had one daughter, but I don't know what happened to her. He never talked about her. Most of everything was business to him. We wondered why he didn't leave everything to her. Maybe they were estranged or maybe she had passed away, too. There was no way of getting in touch with her to tell her about his passing.

—⁂—

Andy was thrilled that he was named in Mr. Dyland's will and all the long years of working in the shop was paying off. Now he could do some things that he could never do before. He had spotted a nice house over on Cross Street and could now put a payment down on it. He also felt he had fewer restraints on him. Maybe he thought that he was part owner of the shop. He began to dress in the most expensive suits. He went to the salon to have his hair dyed. He grew a beard and wore the fanciest of hats. The car dealer was happy that he bought the most expensive car on his lot. He flirted with all the ladies who came in the shop; some found this delightful, but some found it an insult. Dad was hopelessly without a clue as how to handle this situation. Their sales began to drop by twenty percent and Dad knew this had to change somehow.

One day Andy was waiting on a nice-looking, blonde woman. He was practicing his wiles on her as he was now accustomed to do with all the ladies. When he was trying shoes on them, he would look up their skirts. Unfortunately her husband overheard him, and it was bad for him. He came from around the aisle and boxed him right on the floor. It caused quite a stir with the customers. This was the last straw for dad.

"I have to give you your percentage of the sales, but it doesn't mean that you have to work here. Your behavior recently is abhorred. I am the owner of this store and unless you straighten up, you don't work here anymore," Dad said.

I think this got his attention. His playboy days here were over. Maybe it was a middle-age crisis. He came back to work the next day with a completely different attitude, fearing for his job.

The farm and my work at the hospital took up most of my time. I didn't have any social life to speak of. Dad, Mary, and her husband would come over for dinner, or we would go out to eat sometimes. I had to stay busy, and I was fortunate that I did have the farm and work. But there were the nights when I couldn't control my thoughts of my child and husband. I still cried myself to sleep. I missed those cute little chuckles that Manning made when he saw a butterfly or when he would say, "Mummy, I love you." I missed those sweet little kisses that he would place on my cheek. I missed Johann's loving arms around me at night as he cuddled close to me. I missed sharing everything with him. I had learned so many things from him, not just in the medical field but also about living life. What hurt so much was what he did. It was dumfounding, because I knew that he loved life so much. I do know that the human mind is so complex. With all my training in mental health, I did not think that I would have something so heartbreaking in my own family. I wasn't prepared, and it was just too close.

Brett was doing a good job on the farm. He was almost finished fixing the fences. We always had a meeting after he finished one chore and was ready to start another. I was having a hard time figuring out how to best run a farm, as of course, I had never done it before. I grew up on one, but it was not like owning one and being responsible for it. Maybe we should plough up the fields first and get ready for the spring planting as winter was coming. I had heard that one should plough just before the first frost and turn up the roots of the weeds. This way, the heavy frost would kill them. Brett thought this was a good idea to do next.

The next discussion was when to purchase the cattle. Brett had already fenced the fields for planting. The cattle range, catch pens, barn and all were ready. If we bought them now, they would be cheaper, but we would have to feed them through the winter. If we bought them in the spring, they would be at a much higher price. We could buy calves from the dairies, and although they would have to be bottle fed, they would be very cheap. Some would probably not make it without their mother's milk. We decided to buy the cattle now. Brett had stored the barn full of hay. We just needed to buy some corn. In the spring, we could plant corn for the next winter. Dad could help by advising us on raising cattle.

—⁊⁊—

Mum inherited quite a bit of money from Mr. Dyland, and she wondered why he wanted her to have it. She thought that maybe it was because he didn't have any relatives as he had never mentioned any. Anyway, she redecorated their house and bought Mary a new car. Dad needed to do some renovating on the store and purchase new stock. Chain stores were beginning to pop up everywhere, and so he had to compete. Mum was a generous person. She didn't mind sharing her wealth. She had never had so much, and she was always filling the streeters tin cup full and giving them bags of food. A plan for a soup kitchen was in the works and she was just hoping that her health would hold out long enough for it to be built.

Jane Williams and her son, James, would visit me at the farm. Little James loved to ride the pony and pet all the animals. She never asked me to babysit anymore, but she knew that I loved James and enjoyed their visit. She asked me if I needed anyone else to help on the farm. She thought that I might need another hand to clean the house or work the fields and cattle. I had sort of been thinking that I might have to have someone else to help and I probably would need someone to help with the housework as I wasn't ready to retire from the hospital yet. I didn't know much about Jane. I just thought that she was a nice person, a good mother, and a worker in Mary's shop. She knew of a young man named Perry Jones. Actually she had been seeing him for a couple of months. She said that he seemed to be a nice guy and that he was looking for work. I kept that in mind.

The days and night seemed to melt into each other. The soft summer days seemed to become a blur as the evening winds began to get cooler. The green meadows with their swaying leaves were turning red and yellow and falling across the fields like sailing birds embarking in flight. Gone were the blooms of the wild flowers that blanketed the hills. I knew they were scattering their seeds in preparation for their spring embarkment. I pulled my sweater closer around me as I walked through the forest of this land of God. I had always marveled at such greatness of the vast trees and streams. The green ferns were growing along the banks of the creek and the wild purple violets that would bloom in the spring always caught my attention as I followed the path of the creek. I listened as a hawk took flight over my head. I could see where the wild animals had dug their homes in the soft ground. I saw some squirrels and chipmunks scouring around with hickory nuts in their mouths. I could smell the autumn air in my nostrils, and I was alive in this mansion of nature. I sighed as I looked up in the sky of billowing, fluffy white clouds, and it took my breath away.

I hired Perry as our interview with him turned out pretty good. He had been a soldier in the war and had just been hopping from job to job. Many of the city residents had moved to the countryside and needed farm labor. I was hoping that he didn't have a clouded past, but we decided to give him a try.

The cattle were set to arrive that morning. We had decided to increase our heard of beef cattle by a hundred. The trailers were arriving one by one, and we were excited as they were let into the pasture. I was amazed at all the bellowing they did. I guess cows get excited, too, whenever their environment is changed. I knew that I would probably get attached to the calves that would come, but I also knew that I could not do this because they would eventually have to go for sale. I was going to purchase a couple more horses next week. Now I felt like I really owned a sure-enough farm and I wanted to think that Mr. Dyland was looking down on me and was proud and thankful that I was really taking care of his beloved estate.

Now my life was not all work and heartache. I thought this would be the perfect time for a party in this beautiful place. All my coworkers were invited as well as some friends and customers from Dad's and Mary's shops. We planned for weeks on end and Andy, Perry, Jane, and Mary helped with everything. Lights were strung all around the patio and down the driveway. I had a lady from the local pastry shop to do the food. Party decorations were everywhere and an orchestra was set to play till the wee hours. I felt so happily blessed. Our guests dressed in their party attire were everywhere, and they were dancing, mingling, and having a great time. I requested that the band play "Always." It was the song that was playing when Johann first made love to me, and when I became his woman and fell more madly in love with him. Tears came to my eyes as I was back in that room that smelled of bamboo and cedar with rain falling softly. I could see the glimmering of the candle light in the corner of the room. I could even feel the longing for him. I could feel his arms around me and his touch. I wondered if I ever could respond that way again to another man, for it had been a long, long time.

CHAPTER 7

I had been raised in the Catholic Church, but we only went there occasionally. We just knew that the Bible was a roadmap for our lives and it taught us all we needed to know about being good people, and we lived our lives according to it. It's worked out good for us, and I thank God for it and all of his many blessings that he has bestowed upon us. It's kept me out of that deep black hole where no one ever wants to go but some get drawn into, some are on the very edge, and some fall all the way in. I had been taught to always pray for these children of God who had lost their way. Some were so lost that not even prayer and counselling could help them. Their poor lost souls were placed in the hands of the Lord.

I was beginning to realize that Mum was showing signs of being lost. She was diagnosed by the doctor as having hardening of the arteries. Some days she was fine and some days she was talking way out of her mind. It was a wait-and-see daily situation. She would talk about the Lord forgiving her of her sins and she wanted forgiveness from her family. Forgiving her for what? To me she was the most virtuous of women, the best wife to my father, and the best mother to Mary and me. The mind is very mysterious, and all my training and experience as a psychologist could not give me a clue of understanding about her. We just knew that we would give her all the love and understanding we could possibly give her.

A good thing for Mum was that she was able to see the soup kitchen completed and in operation. I won't forget the look on her face when the first line of people came in. They were served vegetable beef soup with crackers and chocolate cake, and the choices available to them for drink were tea, water, or milk. She had tears running down her face. I thought she would fall to the floor. Standing beside her, I felt her lean against me for support. She vowed that as long as her money held out, it would always be used to feed the homeless. She had set up a trust fund that would, if properly run, support the kitchen for many years to come. In her off days, she said that the soup kitchen was one way to help with her repentance.

Perry, the new ranch hand, was doing a great job on the farm. He seemed to have a knack with the horses. He and Brett rounded up some wild horses out on the flats, when I had no idea that we could ever tame them. He knew exactly how to break them to be able to ride them. Mostly, he talked to them and petted them. I called him the horse whisperer. We didn't need very many horses, for all we needed were some to ride and round the cattle up. Now I didn't have to buy any. This was a cattle farm.

We did grow corn and alfalfa for the farm animals. Vegetables were grown so we would have fresh ones for ourselves to eat. For fruits, we had apple, peach, plum, and pear trees. I loved to watch everything grow each spring and smell the sweet smell of the fruit-tree blossoms, and I couldn't resist cutting a few for the house.

Our flower gardens were spectacular! They lined the long driveway to the entrance of the house. There were fountains surrounded by statues of angels and flowering shrubs. A fishing pond was on the side, and it ran around to the back of the house. Brett and Perry liked to catch fish for our dinner sometimes. They had a special iron pot in which they could cook outside over a hot fire and it was fun watching them. I was so glad that they worked and played well together.

My life seemed to be almost perfect if not having to worry about Mum. I knew she was only going to get worse, and it was something that I had to accept. Despite all I had, this beautiful life carved out for me, I was still a lonely woman. I prayed that may God send me someone like Johann to love me, whom I could love back. So far, no one had arrived. *Maybe no one would ever arrive.* I thought. Life was beginning to get shorter as I asked the Lord to please just send me some kind of a sign.

Dad was beginning to find it harder to take care of Mum, and he wasn't in very good health himself. They hired a male nurse who had the strength to lift her in and out of her wheel chair. A housekeeper and cook, too, were hired to help, because Dad wasn't a very good cook. Mum went crazy at the mere mention of a nursing home; no, no, not for her. I visited her when I could or when one of the caretakers had to be off for some reason or another. Hearing that Mum had been wailing, asking for forgiveness from the Lord broke my heart. I asked what she had done to be forgiven for. She would look at me straight in the face and become completely silent. It seemed to be a buried secret deep in her mind for only her to know.

I walked into my parents' house one morning and heard a familiar tune playing in the parlor. I never knew dad had that record. I stopped, still astounded at hearing the melody of "Always." I asked Dad when did he get it, and he said that it was Grayson's, the nurse. I had not met him yet, since he mostly covered the day shift and I usually didn't arrive till late evening after work. It was my day off that day, and hence I came early. I rounded the corner to Mum's room and there he was! Just with the very sight of him, I found myself with the taste of chocolate in my mouth. Was this the sign I had asked God for? What were the chances of someone playing that song? Why did I taste chocolate? It sounds silly, I know, but could it be true? He had salt-and-pepper hair, blue eyes, muscled frame, and average height. I guesstimated him to be about forty-five years old, and he had the look of a patient and gentle man. Dad introduced us, and we said our howdy dos. I knew at that very moment, standing there before God and Dad, that he was the one whom God had chosen for me as my next and last husband here on this earth, Grayson McDonald. We starred at each other for a few moments, as if taking in the sight of each other. His gaze followed me as I kissed Mum on her cheek and as I moved around the room. This moment in time would stick in my memory for the rest of my life.

—⁂—

It is my profession, and once I entered in this line of work, I could never keep myself from analyzing everyone around me. Their body language was always a giveaway, and the expression on their face and even the way they carried themselves was definitely a sign of their well-being, or the opposite. Gradually, Perry began to lie around more and more. This put more work pressure on Brett. However, Brett would not complain unless it was more than he could possibly handle. This was going on too long and it had to be addressed at our weekly farm meeting. We had to have a discussion with Perry. Was it something physical or emotional? The usual plans for the next week and the problems we had had with various things in the past week were always discussed. One of the problems was the problem with Perry. I asked him if he was feeling unwell or if it was a personal problem. I told him that he had to pull his weight on the farm because Brett could not handle the entire workload, but he was reluctant to discuss anything and was reluctant to admit that anything was wrong. We told him that he was like family to us and he had been an excellent farm hand. Whenever anything was going wrong with any of us, we would all stick together and try to figure out the best solution as how to deal with it. He broke down and was shaking in his pants. Finally he said, "I'm scared, scared for me and scared for both of you." Why he was so scared, we wondered. He told us that he had witnessed a murder, and the murderer saw him and knew who he was. That was why he was here asking for work and that Perry was not his real name. He had been running for a year now, not staying at one spot for long, hoping that he could elude the guy. Well, he had seen the guy in town last week, but the guy did not see him. He said that he was so happy working here, but he was also afraid that he would have to move on. *What could I say to this?* I asked myself. *Should I talk to the law?* This was a precarious situation.

I kept mulling this over and over in my mind. What would be the best way to handle this? I came to the conclusion that I would talk to the law and get an artist to come to the farm and do a composite drawing of the guy. Since Perry was not going back to the city for supplies anymore, I didn't think he was in any danger. I thought I would send him off camping on a weeklong inspection of our fences over on the back end of the ranch since our monthly inspection was coming due. This would take the chance of coming in contact with anyone. Yes, I thought this was the best thing to do.

The sketch was done and relayed back to the sheriff's department. All the lodging places and restaurants were checked first. They all said that there was a guy asking about a fellow named John Gallahan, and he did look like the sketch that was drawn by Perry. Bingo, the third one they checked turned up that he was staying there. Then a watch was set up in order to apprend him. Later in the day he was arrested as he entered the hotel. Now Perry could have some peace of mind and would be so relieved when he got back. Upon hearing of the news, Perry's attitude changed drastically, and he told us that he was so thankful for our help.

CHAPTER 8

I thought maybe since things around me were on a steady level—Mum seemed to be holding her own for now; things at the farm were going well; Perry was back and happy; although Dad wasn't feeling at his best, but he was still able to help with Mum; and I had vacation time at the hospital—a mini vacation would do me a world of good, ordered by me, the doctor. The New York's World Fair was being planned to take place and I couldn't think of a better time to go there. I had heard that the Broadway shows were spectacular, and I would have loved to see them. I hadn't shopped for clothes or anything in a very long time, and I had dreamed of the new fashions. Yes, New York, here we come. I was so excited.

I had asked Mary to go with me. She wondered if we both should go away from home, leaving Mum and Dad in bad health, but I knew that if we didn't go now, we certainly wouldn't be able to go any time later. Mum and Dad had the help of Grayson and Eva, the housekeeper, and we wouldn't be gone for more than three weeks.

We booked passage on the Conard White Star Queen Mary ship, one of the most luxurious ships. Many celebrities were known to use her as their main travel. Later she became a war ship and was stripped of her fine furnishings and was named The Grey Ghost. After the war, she had resumed her name, and now it was thought to be haunted. Being on the sea was always our greatest adventure while we were growing up. Tickets were already purchased for the play, "*Oklahoma*" and musicals by Irving Berlin and

Cole Porter. Our excitement could not be contained. Just thinking about shopping at Bloomingdales brought smiles to our faces. We had only a week to pack before sailing. Did I say pack? We're not going to pack very much, because we were going to have to have room to bring back what we bought.

Even with all my excitement about the trip, I could not get Grayson out of my mind. The vision of him for the first time kept popping up at my every turn. I had even dreamed of him kissing me. Dreams of Johann had dominated my dreams for years now. Some of my dreams were sensual, but some were nightmares, and dreams of Manning were especially tormenting to me. The reality of such nights would leave me so listless the next day that I found it hard to function. Yes, I was alone with no one to comfort me and no one to share my thoughts and feelings with. I struggled to keep a positive mind and this I had to do for survival. As they say, *"Tomorrow is another day."* I had a lot to be thankful for. I was very thankful for the life I had ahead of me, and I intended not to waste it.

I had to work quickly to get everything covered at the ranch and I was so blessed that Brett and John, now that we knew Perry's actual name, were very dependable. I outlined the work schedule as far as I needed, but I shouldn't have, because they knew how and when to take care of things or any problems that might pop up. I dreaded leaving my barnyard pets and my dog and cat. I was even thinking that I must be out of my mind, leaving this beautiful place, but there was a great big world out there and I could not wait to see it.

I made one last visit to Mum and Dad before we left, and everyone seemed to be holding their own. They had everything they needed and wanted us to have a good time and to not worry about them. Grayson was as congenial as ever toward me, but I noticed that his eyes followed me everywhere I went, and, I have to admit that mine followed him, too. I could taste that sweetness of chocolate again.

Since the Thames River is an inland waterway and cannot accommodate a large ship, Mary and I had to catch a train to South Hampton for a two-hour ride. We thought maybe it would take seven or more days before arriving in London. We had never been on a passenger ship before, and we were like two kids on a secret journey. Maybe we wouldn't be accosted by pirates or maybe there wouldn't be any mutiny among the crew. Would it be flying a skull flag? We giggled and were eager to check out every nook and cranny we were allowed to go into.

I thought we would get seasick, but the ship's ride was smooth, and we enjoyed being on the deck with the cool sea breeze blowing on our faces. The seagulls would fly by with their whiteness shining like fleeting clouds and making their resounding bird calls. The water was like sparkling diamonds all around us and I was so amazed at such purity of God's beauty. Tears of thankfulness ran down my sun-kissed face and I would never forget this very moment in time in my life.

Meals served were the best. I had to admit that I ate some things that I had never eaten before and most of the time we didn't know what we were eating. Even the most ordinary food was prepared so fancy that it was unrecognizable. It was pure luxury to us to not to have to cook and do housework. Everything was at our command, and we were spoiled royally. There was a museum and a swimming pool with cool inviting water. We met a lot of celebrities, Fred Astaire, Paul Draper, Gene Kelly, and Bing Crosby, among a few others, and we had no idea that the Queen would be sailing on this very ship to New York, too, for the World's Fair. There was a lot of great entertainment from plays to musicals and dancing, and we wondered why we had never done this before.

We arrived in June of 1939 at the King George V. Graving Dock to board the Royal Yacht to New York Harbor. There seemed to be a different feeling to the air from England and a different smell. Maybe it was because we had inhaled the salty sea breezes for so long. America, finally we arrived to a new land to stand our feet on. What a great adventure, and we were just starting.

We had reservations at the Roosevelt Hotel. When we arrived, we weren't disappointed. As we said to each other, "Wow." Exploring every nook and cranny was going to be an experience in itself.

Mary and I were wondering what the women were wearing here. We were going to be dressed differently from them. *Would they notice?* We thought. *What kind of hats and shoes were in style here?* We had been dreaming of shopping where the shops had models to model the new fashions. Their hair styles probably were different, too. New York was heralded as being the capital of high fashion, well, we were ready to find out. Would anyone recognize us in our new clothes and hairstyles when we arrived back home? We knew we would have lots of adventures to talk about.

The World's Fair lived up to our expectants and more. We had never dreamed that it would be like that and almost more than we could take in. It was so massive and covered so much territory that it was astounding. The opening slogan was "The Dawn of a New Day, The World of Tomorrow." It was the second most expensive one and we believed it. We didn't know that it was formed and planned by policeman. They believed that the country needed to have hope and expectations of a better world to live in among all the turmoil suffered, and what a great plan it was!

By 3 p.m. we were drained and needed to eat lunch. We ate in the Schaeffer Center, just one of the largest restaurants at the fair. Their meals ranged from one dollar and thirty-five cents to two dollars and seventy-five cents. It was comparable to an upscale steak house and was delicious. We couldn't believe that all of the tables full of every kind of food imaginable could be arranged in so many different ways. The displays were out of this world with color and fragrances, and, needlessly to say, we didn't go hungry.

We caught a cab to the hotel and immediately conked out. The next day we had to shop for some of those high fashions we had been so looking forward to buying. Mary wanted to get some ideas about ordering different styles for her shop. I just wanted to admire them and buy some for myself and maybe some things that Mum might need.

I woke up with a start. I had been having a dream about a man. As I began to wake up more, I realized that it was a dream about Grayson. It was a dream that you are ashamed to tell anyone about. Why, with all my excitement and planning of our trip, I hadn't thought about anything like that, but I always heard that your dreams show you what was in your subconscious mind. I had not been with a man since Johann. I always tried to put sex out of my mind. But this dream had awakened feelings that I thought were long gone. I began to remember how wonderful it was to have a man's arms around me and to feel his tender kiss and touch. I was already looking forward to returning home to see Grayson again and to taste that decadent chocolate. I wondered what the future held for us, if anything.

Mary and I were up and running with a quick breakfast in the hotel and off we were to the shops today. Many people were already crowding the streets. There were so many shops that we didn't know which one to go in first, so we chose one that modeled the fashions. Mary wanted to pick out the ones she wanted to order through wholesale. The models were outstandingly beautiful, and it got Mary to think about having fashion shows in her shop. I thought it was a wonderful idea. There were just as beautiful girls in England as in New York. The accessories were far more stylish than we had and all different from any we had ever seen. The fashion jewelry was made of colorful beads, shiny stones, and so many designs. I never knew that hats could be made in so many different ways. The shoes were of diverse styles, but I thought some would be difficult to walk in. Shop after shop had different merchandise, and we were beyond excited.

We had worn ourselves out and worked up an appetite, so we stopped at a little outside patio restaurant with tables covered in bright colored table clothes and umbrellas. Vibrant flowers of yellow and white surrounded the brick fence. A fountain was in the center with water spraying like rhinestones and cascading over a mermaid, and I could feel a soft mist on my face. One of Cole Porter's songs was playing "Midnight Stars and You" by Ray Noble and Al Bowly. I listened to the words. It was strange that I never realized I was so lonely at that very moment, among all the people and excitement. What was so different? Had the dream I had dreamed the night before stirred up all the feelings I had suppressed all these years?

We visited more and more shops that day. Walking on the crowded streets, Mary suddenly stopped and pointed at a man.

"It's him!" she said. I asked myself, *Whom would she know here?*

"Who?" I asked.

"It's Daniel."

I directed my brain to figure who was Daniel. Bingo, he was the man in her continuing dreams. Oh, no!

She began running toward him. He had a beautiful, red-haired, stylish-looking woman on his arm. I ran after her and grabbed her by her shoulder.

"Mary you can't be serious."

"Anna, let me go. I know it's him."

I couldn't hold her. She ran after them, and I ran after her. They had slipped in one of the night clubs and were out of sight. We went into the first one but they were nowhere to be found. Good thing.

Mary was beside herself, insisting that he was Daniel. I tried to tell her that lots of people look alike and anyway Daniel was just a figment of her elusive dreams. She said she knew him and he was real to her. I knew then that Mary needed more counselling, and I was afraid if she was falling back into that secret imaginary life that only she knew and lived.

The next morning, we went back to the fair to enjoy the many displays and awesome everything, but Mary was a little subdued all day. She kept looking for Daniel and hoping that she would see him again. I was hoping she wouldn't, and I wondered what would happen if she did. I thought it would be pretty embarrassing to all three of us or all four of us if he still had his girlfriend or wife. I would hate to have to cut our trip short if she got out of hand, I would have to use all my skills as a psychologist to help her.

On our third day, we decided to see some of the countryside, so we had a picnic basket packed to go out on Long Island. The island is a point thirty-five miles from Manhattan. One of the hotels' management encouraged us not to go to there, because there were rumors of Nazi camps disguised as family and youth camps. They had recreational activities, but with a German flair. It was really focused on the children to be trained as little Aryans in the thoughts of taking over the country. There was forced sex in order to produce more Aryans, and many of the campers were sexually attacked. We were grateful for the information and decided not to go there, but to go to Central Park.

We were so amazed with everything; it was almost too much to take in. By the end of the day, we were so tired that we ate a light dinner at our hotel and went immediately to bed. I awoke by Mary talking to someone, and as I came to full awareness, I realized that she was dreaming. What was I going to do to help her get over her continuing dreams of Daniel? Hypnosis had helped her before, maybe it would help her again. I was hoping that she wouldn't see that man who she said was him again this day, for tomorrow would be our last day before sailing home.

The next day we boarded the tour bus, for it was just impossible to see everything on our own and go everywhere. What a wonderful trip we were having and we hated for it to end. We found our seat on the third row; all the other seats were filling up fast. I noticed that Mary had become excited as I watched her face turn red. I couldn't believe it.

She whispered to me, "He just passed by us, it's Daniel. I have to speak to him, he's real."

"Mary, please," I said, "It's just a figment of your imagination."

She would not be convinced, and this time he was alone. As we were at the end of our tour and everyone began embarking off the bus, Mary stopped and waited as one by one each of the tourists stepped off. I didn't know what to do, I knew she was determined to stop and talk to this man. What was she going to say to him, "I've been dreaming about you for a long time, we've been together sexually, I know you and you should know me, we've had a life together?" Oh, would he think she was a crazed woman? I tried to get her to not stop, and we had to catch a cab back to the hotel, but she would not be swayed.

I watched as he stepped down from the bus. About thirtyish, I guessed, blonde hair combed neatly back. He was of medium build, dressed in fashionable clothes and expensive-looking, shiny shoes, and close shaven.

Mary called to him, "Sir, may I have a word with you, please?"

He looked her way, and the two locked eyes in what seemed a long moment, each having a questioning look on their faces, yet looks of familiarity. I stood there bewildered, what in the world was happening here.

People of all kinds were scattering everywhere, looking at their next tour schedules. We were the only ones stopped dead in our tracts. I didn't know what to say. Was Mary going to make a spectacle of herself?

"Are you Daniel?" she asked.

"As a matter of fact, I am," he answered. "You look familiar, but I can't quite place you. Wait, give me a minute. I never forget a face. You're someone from my childhood. Are you from London?"

"Yes, I am," Mary responded. "Okay, I can't remember your name, but I know your face, how could I forget the first girl I ever kissed. We must have been about four years old. I think I asked you to marry me. Gosh, amazing, meeting you here and meeting you again after all these years."

Mary could not say a word. She just looked at him. I thought she was going to faint. *I* could not say a word. My mind was whirling in disbelief. Daniel *was* a real person! When we all got our composure, we all decided to stop into a small coffee shop and visit.

Again with all my psychology training, I had never had a case of this nature, and I had truly learned just how complex the human mind can be. My own sister was a lesson well learned. I knew her dreams had to be connected to something. Problems of the mind almost always stem from childhood. Although hers weren't bad experiences, they were so deep seated in her subconscious mind that she had taken on the continuation of Daniel marrying her and living happily together through her dreams. I wasn't sure if we should have told Daniel about her dreams of him. I was hoping that Mary would realize now how and why her obsession over her dreams came about.

I sat and watched them talk about when they were children. Mary didn't remember him in her conscious mind until Daniel reminisced about their school teacher and one time when she had come from the bathroom with toilet tissue trailing from under her skirt. Daniel was married to the red-haired lady we had seen him with the day before. They had two beautiful children, and they lived in South Hampton. Mary told him about her husband and her career as a shop owner in London. Maybe this would put an end to her dream relation with him. Who knows? Only time could take care of this. They finished their talk, and we began our trek back to the hotel.

I wasn't going to bring up the subject of Daniel. Experience had taught me to always let the patient talk about what they felt most comfortable talking about. I realized this was a different case, and Mary wasn't officially my patient, since we were related. She didn't talk about it. We had dinner and went straight to bed, but I knew that she would talk when she was ready. I, myself, had a study report case to write about in the medical journal. I was hoping it would be of some help to the medical field in the cases of dreams and the human mind.

—ɯ—

We were up early the next morning to board the ship back home. Being on the ship was almost as exciting and fun as New York. Mary commented that she truly felt like the real Queen Mary, being on such a luxurious boat. Needless to say that we both didn't know that this was to be one of the last trips it would make as a passenger ship.

Within about three months after our trip on September 3, 1939, England declared war on Germany. They had invaded Poland, Czechoslovakia, Rhineland, and Austria. This had gone on since 1931, because Japan wanted to expand their territory by seizing their land for supplies of oil and rubber.

England's entry into the war was forced by the German Nazi ruler, Adolf Hitler. He was a nonstop aggressive war monger who was evil, a cold-hearted murderer, and would do anything to accomplish his goal. England was in the position on the western front line against the Germans. The United States and England joined together to protect Great Britain. Neville Chamberlain was the prime minister at the beginning of the war, but he was replaced in May 1940 by a more aggressive prime minister, Winston Churchill.

The Queen Mary was converted to a war ship. She was painted a navy gray and was renamed The Grey Ghost. Her elegant furnishings were stripped and stored in warehouses and the port holes were painted over. She was chosen because of her speed and because she posed less of a target because she could sail at a speed of 28.5 knots. She could accommodate a whole Army troop in one voyage.

After the end of the war in 1947, the Queen was converted back into a passenger ship and restored to her former elegant furnishings. She continued to make the two-week Atlantic crossing between South Hampton to New York and Cherbourg till its retirement in 1967.

Everyone was at low ebb. The First World War hadn't been that long ago and now we were facing another war. What were we going to do now? Businesses were going to go bankrupt. We hadn't fully rebounded after the fall of the 1929 stock market. It came as a complete surprise to investors. The government and businesses hoped that it would pass, but they stood by watching it slide deeper into the worst depression of all time.

Arriving back home was a bitter–sweet occasion for Mary and me. The rumors of the impending war came as a consuming threat to our lifestyle as we knew it. We had a lot to think about to prepare if anyone could prepare for such a horrifying war that was to follow. We knew we had to think about Mum and Dad first, and we knew we had to get everyone out of the city. We knew what war could do to our city and our people. We had to pray and pray hard. LORD HELP US!

Our family was in a lot better place than most people who lived in the city. My ranch was outside of London city where most of the infrastructure damage would most certainly be. Mr. Dyland had built a bunker concealed under a garden, which could house a dozen people. He had learned from the last war and meant to be prepared for another. It had all sorts of bottled and canned food, wine, juices, and water. He had thought of everything one might need for survival. Thank you, Mr. Dyland. Mary packed most of her stock in her shop and stored it away. Dad and Andy did the same thing at their store. We moved Mum and Dad out to the farm and needed Grayson to come, too, to help with Mum. He was glad to come since he had no family to be concerned about. The bunker could house all of our family and ranch hands. Freshly washed clothing, blankets, and fuel for the heat source was our concern now since winter was approaching. We knew that if we didn't stock up now, then there wouldn't be any. For meat, we butchered some of our livestock and smoked and bottled it, and we also gathered what we could in the garden and bottled it.

Petrol began to be rationed in September of that year, 1939. Food was rationed in 1940. Seventy percent of London's food supply was imported. It was not a free market anymore but was controlled by a centralized control and planning board. Everyone had food ration books to be able to purchase sugar, meat, cheese, and fats. We were asked to save all our tin cans for the war effort to make ammunition.

Businesses were closing and residents of the city were hustling to get out to the countryside. Some had already fled on the Queen Mary to America on her last voyage. In September 1940, London suffered aerial bombardment to their commercial and residential districts, the heart of the city, when 30,000 died and 50, 00 were injured. Because of the nightly air raids a "BLACK OUT" began in the city, which had to remain dark. A fine was imposed on anyone who even lit a match. Later illuminated signs and glimmer star lighting was permitted. Many road accidents occurred as a result, because some were trying to travel at night with no lights.

We all lived in and out of the bunker. Mum was getting worse. She was good some days, but others were a nightmare for us. Someone had to keep an eye on her at all times, because she would wander into the woods, and winter was here. We were afraid that she would get lost and freeze to death. She would talk out of her head a lot. Mostly all her rantings were about forgiveness from us and her sister. As far as we knew, she didn't even have a sister. Even though her mind was fragile, she seemed to be healthy otherwise. It was another story with Dad, he had high blood pressure, and all the conditions we were living with were like adding fuel to a fire. Grayson had to take care of him, too, but he never complained.

We lived day by day listening for air raids. Most were in the distance toward the city. Many people were seen wandering down by the road, and some came to the house begging for food and water. I just could not refuse them. I gave them enough for a meal, but I had to send them on their way. I had plenty of milk from the cows and gave them a gallon each. Eventually there were so many of them that Perry, I still called him Perry, and Brett had to put up a locked gate. I felt so bad for having to do that that I put out what I could at the entrance. If I didn't have anything else, I had beef, milk, and water from the well.

It was very cold one night, and the bombing seemed to have ceased. Mum and Dad had had a good day, and they were sleeping sound. Through all the problems of our situation, we still had to take time for some peace in our lives. Joy had been a stranger to us since we got off the Queen Mary over a year ago. With everyone constantly around, I still was lonely. The thoughts and memories of Johann constantly were on my mind and I still couldn't understand why he left me, too. Feeling guilty for Manning's death just was too much for him. I was mad at him. Why couldn't he understand what it would do to me to lose them both? I could not forget how his arms felt around me and how passionate his kisses were. I missed sharing the events of the day and just sitting beside him. I missed his warm hand on mine. I missed planning our future together. I missed that intimacy that a man and a woman shared.

I didn't want anyone to see the tears I couldn't hold back like the tears I had cried so many times before, so I went into the house. Thinking about my little Manning and his sweet face and soft little hands reaching for me was just too much. I heard the screen door creak as Grayson entered the room. We had gotten so caught up with taking care of Mum and Dad and trying to survive the war that we hadn't thought about each other. Noticing the tears, he put his arms around me and held me close. The warmth of his body filled me with emotions and awoke the woman inside me; the woman that I had forgotten existed. His lips found mine and I yielded to their softness. Suddenly I forgot about the war, survival, even Mum and Dad, and the sadness in my soul. His lips became more urgent, and he held me tighter. I could feel his hardness and the moisture between my legs. The whisper of long denied love for me was on his lips and I couldn't deny that I had loved him from the very first day we met. Our lovemaking was so unexpected, but I felt so loved and complete again. I had that delicious taste of chocolate again.

I knew Grayson was a good man by the way he took care of Mum and Dad, and he was gentle, kind, and dedicated to his profession. Living together with everyone in close quarters was like a family, and we all helped each other get through this terrible time in history. We prayed that this war would soon be over and we could get back to our normal lives. We could hear the air raid sirens in the distance and were thankful but still heartbroken that most of the bombings were in the city and people lost their lives and businesses.

Many of the electrical lines were down and communication was low, but we did have one of the first battery-operated radios. There was the MOI, Ministry of Information, a government department, in the senate building at the University of London. They were responsible for the publicity and propaganda of the war, and we were able to keep up with the sad condition of the world.

I talked about all the things that were rationed before, but one of the things I now think about and smile. We ladies had to do anyhow and anyway we could. Although the rationing of clothes didn't affect us since we had owned clothing shops, many ladies could not buy silk stockings. Being creative, they would tan their legs and draw a seam down them. Fabric was rationed and this brought about a fashion change. Lot of cotton material was used in parachutes, which created a shortage. Skirts were made shorter in order to save material. Children's toys were hard to find; they had to find ways to make their own. I remember the spool dolls, the toy trucks, and the cars made out of wood. Of course the rag dolls were popular that were made out of scrap cloth. Soap and washing powder were rationed and many made homemade soap out of lye and fat. We used that old iron wash pot a lot with a fire built around it. Mum had washed our clothes in it using a rub board and bluing was used to make our white clothes whiter. That old wash pot sure did cook some good peanuts, too. We would invite the neighbors and have a peanut boil. Sorghum syrup was made out of the juice of sugar cane, and we used it in place of sugar. There was a round bin that, when filled up with the juice, was cooked to a certain temperature. A mule was harnessed and somehow had the cane hooked so that when he walked round and round the bin, it squeezed out the juice into the bin which had a fire built around it and it was cooked to a certain syrupy temperature. Someone had to try to keep the pesky yellow jackets away which were drawn to the sweet nectar.

As time went on, the war was beginning to wind down and we began to find out just what a horrible war it was. Hitler was a monster, and we heard what he did to the Jews. We couldn't believe the murders and atrocities of poor, innocent men, women, and children. They would steal their riches and do medical experiments on their bodies. Mum wanted to attend mass services and we all felt like we should, too, to pray for them and give thanks for our rich blessings.

CHAPTER 9

Everyone knew by now that Grayson and I were in love. Being in love is fun and magical, and it is the most euphoric feeling one can experience. We always enjoyed being together and doing things together. There was a special spot on the ranch beside the lake we believed God made just for us. We would take a picnic lunch and watch the fish jump up and the squirrels search for hickory nuts. It was a good place away from everybody to discuss and plan our marriage. We both knew that soon in the near future we would be married and share the rest of our lives together.

Mary and Harvey eventually went back to check on their home and Mary's shop. Their home was completely gone and the shop had a lot of damage. They planned to have the shop repaired and opened again. They lived with us till they rebuilt their house. She still had the merchandise stored in our barn, and it was a blessing because of the shortages of everything. Because of Dad's bad health, he sold his shop to Andy. We knew we wouldn't have him much longer as he was beginning to get very frail. Grayson and I got married that spring of 1944. I never have regretted it. I was so blessed with such a good man.

It was 1945 and I was thirty-seven. Germany has finally surrendered and the war has finally ended. London has been left in shambles but like after the first war, they recoup fast. Ships brought skilled workers to rebuild and in 1946 there was a boom to the economy. Heathrow Airport was open again to travel. The Waterloo Bridge was built over the Thames River. I had gone back to work at the hospital, because I knew there would be soldiers that needed me.

Dad died the next month of a heart attack. He was trying to tell me something, but couldn't get the words out. Mum never realized that he wasn't around anymore. Maybe that was a blessing, because they had once been so close to each other. Most days she talked out of her head, mostly about the same things, forgiveness and not being worthy of her blessings. This was still puzzling to us all. On some days, she was downright mean and hard to handle and on other days, she just sat with a blank look on her face and never said a word. I was thankful that she was still eating and drinking, but was finding it hard to get around.

It was a new day and a new world for us. The farm was flourishing and I was counting my blessings that the war was finally over. Everyone was busy cleaning up the streets and their homes. Mary's shop was almost finished. She was busy getting all her merchandise back on the shelves and racks. There was an atmosphere of energy and hope everywhere. Harvey had taken over Mum's soup kitchen. Even though there were jobs for almost everyone, many, many people were still in need of a hot meal, a cot to sleep on, and clothes to wear. Thanks again to Mr. Dyland and Mum. I just wished Mum knew that her venture to help take care of the underprivileged was still in place.

I stopped by the soup kitchen after work one day to see Harvey and to help with anything he might need. An elderly man was there sitting and eating the soup of the day. He was completely white headed and had a long, white beard. He was wrinkled and frail with age. He looked up when I came in and looked at me as though he recognized me. I knew that I had never met him before, but I thought that I must have looked like someone from his past. He smiled and was exuberant as he held out his hand to me.

"Where have you been all these years?" he asked.

I took his soft, warm hand in mind as if I knew him. All I could say was that I had gotten married and still lived in London. I sat down beside him and had a bowl of soup myself. He rambled on about what had been going on in the streets, what the streeters had to do to survive the war, and about many who didn't survive. He named names as if I would remember them. I went along with him, and it seemed to make him happy. I asked him if he needed anything and told him that he was always welcome here and that if he did need anything, Harvey would see that he got it. It just broke my heart to see all the new people here as the results of the war but happy that we could be there for them.

—❧—

Andy had Dad's shop up and running which was his now. He had been part of our family for more years than I could remember, and I liked to stop by and shop for special things for Grayson, because I liked to surprise him and show that I loved him so much. I still couldn't believe that God had matched me with two fine men to be my husbands. Grayson took such good care of Mum, but I could tell that it was taking a toll on him both physically and mentally. We both still had to help manage the ranch, too.

I put in a request to the hospital to cut down my hours at work. It was granted and I was able to stay at home and help more. Perry and Brett did a great job with the cattle and the crops, but they needed more time to do some of their recreational activities and have a life of their own. Brett had met a girl whom he fancied and liked to spend time with. Perry liked to participate in rodeos and horse shows. I knew that in the near future I would lose one of them to seek another lifestyle, but for right now they seemed to still like to be cowboys. This was their home and I loved them like brothers.

The ranch produced a lot of beef, pork, chickens, eggs, and milk, and the fields produced a lot of vegetables. We also raised cotton every year, and we were glad when the cotton picker combine was invented. It had taken a lot of attempts over the years to perfect it. Even though cotton was king for clothing, the war had needed a lighter material for parachutes. Thereby, man-made materials like nylon and other materials were produced. This cut down on the cotton trade for clothing. We were glad we could supply some of our bounty to the soup kitchen to feed the large numbers of homeless people.

As I think of Mr. Dyland, I think that this all could not have been possible without him. It makes my heart warm that he left this ranch to me and I'm so impressed with what Mum did with the money he left her. She was so compassionate and dedicated to her soup kitchen. I know nothing about her childhood since she lost both of her parents to tuberculosis. Mum said they caught it by sleeping on feather pillows. Apparently the feathers were infected with the disease. Some of the family were quarantined and cared for at TB hospitals. She was raised by an aunt, but she, too, died with yellow fever when Mum was fourteen. Shortly afterward, Mum and Dad married. People married young back then and had lots of children to work on their farms. Most farmers borrowed money at the bank or feed stores against their crops, and when their crops were harvested, they paid the loans back.

Nothing about Mr. Dyland's family was known. All we knew was that he ran a prosperous business for years which Dad and Andy worked at. He was well known in London and was on the board of directors at the bank. His home and ranch of thousands of acres were inherited from his parents. We just knew he was always congenial with everyone, even when Andy pulled his shenanigans.

CHAPTER 10

Compassion is the chief law of human existence.
—*Fyodor Dostoevsky*

Mum was getting worse and had to have constant care. She was eating very little and despite all the extra vitamin supplements we gave her, she began to fail both mentally and physically. One day Grayson came into her room to help her into her wheelchair. She had a fireplace poker hidden in her gown and attacked him viciously. She hit him in the face and his lower body before he was able to restrain her. Luckily, I was in the nearby room, heard the commotion, and was able to get to Grayson quickly. His face was bleeding profusely. He had blacked out and was lying on the floor. Mum had a smile on her face. I called for help as I scrambled to the kitchen for cold-water soaked towels to help stop the bleeding. Perry came and stayed with Mum and Brett and I took Grayson to see the doctor. Grayson was in pretty bad shape as the doctor examined him and admitted him to the hospital right away. He had forty-five stitches to his face and had to have surgery to his lower private area. Despite the surgery, he was rendered impotent. He would need all my love and understanding more than he ever needed them. I was there ready to love him and reassure him that the only thing that mattered in our marriage was the love we had for one another. A week later, Mum noticed that Grayson was injured and wondered what had happened to him. We just had to lie to her and tell her that his horse ran into a tree branch.

What to do with Mum now was the question. We removed everything from her room that could be used as a weapon to herself or to anyone else, and we had to keep the door to her room locked. Of course we realized that she was not responsible for her actions, that it was her condition. I just wanted to make sure Grayson thought the same, and he did. We were not the kind of people who would just lock her up forever. She was my mother. We made certain that she was moved around in the house and outside for fresh air and sunshine. Of course, we had to keep her strapped to her wheelchair. We had a physical therapist to come out for her exercises, and we also thought that she wouldn't last much longer in this world.

Three months later, one day when Mum was having one good day out of a lot of bad days, she asked me to have Father John come over and talk to her. I knew I should be hasty about this, because a good day could turn into a bad day any minute. I called Father John and he said he could come that afternoon.

Father John had been our Catholic priest for as long as I could remember. He was not only our priest but also a family friend. He had been a God send in our lives after the death of Manning and Johann and losing Dad. Mum asking for him now gave me an ominous feeling that the end for her was approaching and she knew it.

Seeing the reverend drive up the driveway seemed to me to be an angel coming to collect Mum for heaven. Tears rolled down my face. What was I going to do without her? I could not fathom not seeing her face ever again, even though she had not been herself for years, I just couldn't think of losing her. The strict, but sweet Mum had been locked in another dimension with actions created by a mysterious condition unknown to her. This strange personification of evil had invaded her body and mind to do its dirty work. It had stumped even the best and brightest of medical scientists. I knew not what they discussed. I would have guessed it was about her salvation and her crossing to the other side of the Veil. Would she have been confessing her sins? Could it have been what she was talking about needing to be forgiven by us? Did, I wonder, she say anything about her sister she was raving about—the sister she didn't even have? The sister must have been part of her delirious thinking. I could not ask the reverend what they talked about, for I knew he couldn't divulge any of their conversation. I just hoped she kept a sane mind for the time they talked. We would just have to love her and understand her for what time she may have left. She finally realized one day that Dad wasn't around but thought that he had gone to town and would be back soon with her favorite candy bar.

CHAPTER 11

How far you go in life depends on you being tender with
the young, compassionate with the aged, sympathetic
with the striving, and tolerant with the weak and strong.
Because someday in life you will have been all of these.
—*George Washington Carver*

One morning I looked down the driveway and saw a man walking. Our gates were usually locked, but maybe someone forgot to lock them back. He looked like he was in his forties, maybe, with a beard and a limp. Was he a homeless person looking for work? I didn't know. Dad always taught me to be cautious about strangers, so I grabbed my Saturday night special pistol. He walked around the house to the back door and knocked. Grayson was lying in bed still recovering from Mum's attack. I walked around to the kitchen door and asked who was there.

"I'm Ted Walker, ma'am I'm looking for farm work," he responded.

I walked outside, keeping my pistol in my apron pocket. He had the saddest eyes I had ever seen and his clothes were worn and dirty. His body was thin and frail looking.

"What can you do, are you experienced in farm labor?" I asked.

I said to myself that he probably was too weak to do anything strenuous.

"I can do all of it, work in the fields, round up cattle, I especially can do horse shoeing."

I could see in his eyes that he was desperate for work and needed to eat. The pleading in his voice melted my heart. How could I not help this man? I knew with Grayson's injury that he would not be able to do anything for a long time. I also knew that I did not know this stranger's story yet. So, I called Perry, and he came from the barn.

"Take this man to the bunk house and set him up with a bed." Show him where everything is, the shower, etc. and give him some fresh clothes. Then send him back to the back porch and we can interview him for a job."

"Yes, ma'am," Perry said.

Winter was on its way, and we had lots to do to ready the animals. England's winters could be very vicious and there was a new addition to the end of the barn that needed to be finished. Some hay in the fields was still left to be baled and we could use another hand around here.

From the hungry look in the man's face, I felt like he should be fed before we embarked on his interview. Perry brought him back to the back porch all clean with his hair combed straight back where I had a steaming bowl of soup and corn bread and a glass of milk waiting for him.

"Much obliged," he said as he tore into the hot, fragrant soup. I went back into the house to check on Grayson and Mum before I got started with my interview.

I had never seen anyone that hungry and wondered when he had eaten last. He had three bowls of soup, an iron skillet of corn-bread, and a quart of milk. He then asked me if I had any dessert. I brought out a half of a custard pie. Finally he put his fork down and belched loudly.

"Thank you so much, ma'am, I am so beholding to you."

"You're welcome," I said. "Now let's get down to what you can do for our ranch."

He cleaned up pretty good, and with his belly full the color seemed to be coming back into his face. I felt so bad for the many more like him, women and children and I gave thanks to God for my many blessings.

"Do you have a family? If you do, where are they?" I asked.

"Yes, they're at the shelter in London. I have been looking for work in the countryside for the last three weeks. We had a home close to the river, but it was bombed, and we didn't have the money to rebuild."

"Okay, I want you to get some rest and afterward Brett and Perry will show you around and get you started with the work. We all work around here, and I will have no back talk. We do anything and everything that needs to be done. If you have a problem, feel free to discuss it with me. We are an honest family and I expect you to be honest. We have no thieves here, and if you need anything, ask for it," I replied.

He nodded in confirmation and walked out of the room. I felt in my heart that this was a good man down on his luck. I knew that time would tell what kind of a man he really was.

A month had gone by and our new hand was doing well on the ranch. He had even put on a few pounds and looked much stronger. I was wondering about his family still in the shelter. He had visited them a few times. I called him in one day and asked him about them.

"Yes, ma'am, I have a wife and two children there, and I plan to try to find a house to rent so we can be together again." I told him that there was an old shack on the south forty that could possibly be fixed up to live in. There was a spring he could get water from, but there was no electricity. His eyes lit up. "Oh, I would love to go and check it out if I can."

"Sure, we can ride out with Brett and Perry and get some ideas as to what we'll need to make it livable."

The old shack had been one of many like the ranchers used when there was a cattle drive. They just camped out under the stars most of the nights. If the weather was too cold or rainy, they used the shacks. The fireplace was still in tack, but all the windows needed to be replaced. Luckily, the door had remained closed and animals were kept out except for some field mice. There was nothing that couldn't be taken care of with a lot of cleaning and fixing up.

—∿—

The next day, I visited Dad's grave. We had him buried in the Dyland family cemetery on the hillside overlooking the creek that ran into the lake where the wildflowers waved their pretty heads in the gentle breezes and their bright colors were meant to be seen. In the fall, there was an old oak tree that was determined to be the last of the trees to release its brown leaves, as if it wanted to hold onto them as long as it could. We had a special bench there to sit and talk. Dad loved the forest, the creek, and the lake where he loved to fish. The ducks liked to fly over as if sailing, and then would come to a sudden dive for a flashing fish. The blue herons with their stalk legs nested high atop the pine trees on the small island in the lake, which was the nesting and roosting place for the geese. This was their safe place, free from crawling predators. We would see them come in late in the evening and leave out early in the morning. I loved to hear the honking of the geese and the weird sound the herons made while feeding their young. Nature seemed to be at its best in this perfect spot God had made.

As I sat on the bench atop this hill, I felt closer to heaven there than any other place. I could smell the fragrance of the wild flowers and the pine trees and hear the wind whistling through their branches. A pine cone or two would fall occasionally and catch me off guard, and I would jump. Butterflies flew around hoping to get a sweet taste of nectar. Oh, how beautiful they were! The grass was thick under my feet, and I felt the young grasshoppers scrambling to safety. I thought I heard my Dad's voice whispering softly as the wind caressed the trees. It seems that as time goes by, we seem to find it difficult to completely focus on one's face, but the sound of their voice never leaves us. As I talked to him, I told him about Mum and that she would soon join him. I told him how thankful and blessed I was that he had been my dad and how much I loved him.

—〰—

The world was changing very fast and unemployment was very low in the 1950s. The first supermarket opened in 1948. Before then, you could call a bakery or butcher to order, and a boy on a bicycle would deliver it. That was if you lived in the city. There was still rationing, but food rationing had ended in 1954. Thereafter began a long period of prosperity, and Great Britain was becoming an affluent society and so much was being accomplished in technology. Television was one of the most sought out changes in entertainment after 1941. The world was ready for something other than war and destitution. The war worn people needed something to laugh about and to take their minds off of their problems. Radio had already been invented, but television took the world by a storm, and everybody had to have one. Of course many couldn't afford one and some put up fake aerials to pretend to their neighbors that they did own one. Television was here to stay, and it pushed aside every other medium of entertainment. By 1954, Milton Berle was the personification of television. I bought a TV and it was amazing how it kept Mum calm. I liked it, but I still had to play my old phonograph. I could not give up my easy listening music and especially the song "Always" which was Johann and my song by Frank Sinatra.

It was the late fall of 1954. We dug our bumper crop of peanuts. Party time was calling me. We invited the neighbors for a peanut boil. A fire was built around that old iron wash pot and then filled with peanuts, water, and lots of salt. I can still smell them boiling and I can still taste them. Grayson played the fiddle and Brett played the guitar. I wheeled Mum outside so she could attend the festivities. She seemed to enjoy it as she clapped her hands and laughed as it was a good day for her. Life as we knew it then was getting better and the world was rebounding from the war.

Cars on the roads were increasing by 1959 and about thirty-two percent of households owned a car. The first parking meters were installed in the city in 1958 but women were slow about learning to drive. It just seemed that it was a thing for men to do.

—⟋⟍—

The work on the shack on the south forty was going well and Ted brought his family to meet us and to see the shack. They were a most appreciative family and ready to have a house of their own and to all be together. Living on the streets and the shelter was not a good thing, but thank goodness, they did not go hungry. I could use his wife, Mable, in the house and the kids were old enough to help in the stables with the farm animals. As with the children, they were so excited to see the animals and pet them. I had gotten to know Ted as a good man and thought I again was blessed with good hands to run my ranch.

Grayson was healing physically, but it had taken a toll on him. Not being able to perform as a man had taken away a part of him that he thought was most important to our marriage. I assured him that I loved him unconditionally and we would be fine. Just being with him and doing things together was enough for me, but I knew he thought differently about the total sexual intimacy we couldn't share anymore. Things happen in life that we have no control of, and we just have to accept them and focus on what we have to be thankful for. Being such a good man, he wasn't bitter toward Mum, and I loved him even more for that. It still was a good life for we still shared our dreams for the ranch and the soup kitchen, and we were best friends and did everything together.

—ɯ—

Mary was still busy in her shop, and everything seemed to be going well. Her and Harvey's house was finished. She came to see Mum every week and helped as much as she could. I know she wondered why Mr. Dyland left me the ranch and her what he did, but she never mentioned it. I couldn't understand it myself other than that our family worked in his shop for years and he had no relatives. She never mentioned Daniel anymore either. I think she came to the understanding that all those dreams came from her childhood, and they did, but still it was very unusual.

Ted worked very hard on the shack getting it ready before winter struck. He built a small barn for his horse and wagon. Although automobiles were plentiful, he had not earned the money to buy one yet. He moved his family in, his wife Mable, daughter Eva, and son Peter. I hadn't been around many children especially since Manning. Peter had that sparkle in his eyes that reminded me of Manning. He was a delightful child of six and was just learning his alphabet and numbers. I found myself wanting to teach him everything and he was like a sponge soaking up every little bit of knowledge with all the questions he would ask. His thirst for knowledge was remarkable. This child was drawn to me and me to him. I knew it was not healthy to spend so much time with me, and not with his mother. Eventually his parents began to notice and began to make excuses that he had chores to do and could not visit me so often. I knew myself that it had to be this way, because I realized I was still mourning Manning, and I could not replace him with Peter. The mother in me yearned for a child and I would never have one.

Mable was a god send in the kitchen. She knew how to cook the most scrumptious cakes and pies and her soups and casseroles would rival the most experienced chefs. It was a good thing because we had some men who could eat a whole side of beef. I found her cooking hard to resist, but I had to watch my weight.

She was beginning to become a good friend, too, and I needed a female friend in my life. We liked to discuss the children and their future. I liked to talk about making Eva some pretty dresses because I had the talent for sewing. She would look in the Aldens or Sears Roebuck catalog and pick out the one she liked, and we would go to town and buy the fabric she liked and I would sew one like she picked. I didn't need a pattern. She was so thrilled when I finished one and I liked to see the look on her face as she tried them on.

Mum was still eating, and that was a good thing, and she was still asking what happened to Grayson. Now and then she wondered about Dad and when will he get back from town with her candy bar. I wanted to tell her that Dad was gone and would never get back and that Dad had died. What would it do to her if I told her? She could go either way, be so upset that she would get depressed and would stop eating. Maybe she would forget the next second that I told her so I thought it best not to tell her. Each day was an adventure with her and not necessarily a good one. Sometimes she could be innocently funny and if we laughed, she would have that questioning look on her face. I felt bad when I laughed and she couldn't understand why I was laughing. This disease she had was devastatingly puzzling. It was a robber of brain cells and dignity and the everyday quality of life.

Brett came in one morning and announced to me that he was getting married. I was horrified that he would be leaving the ranch. He had met a lady in town who had completely stolen his heart.

"Are you leaving the ranch?" I asked.

"Oh, no, ma'am," he said.

He had saved up enough money to buy a fine automobile and could drive back and forth. She had a house close to the city and he would be moving there. I asked him to bring her to the ranch to meet me. I knew that sooner or later I would be losing one of them, or both. They had been loyal workers for me for a long time, and the ranch would not be the same without them.

Perry was still Perry as I still called him. I loved him like a younger brother and I believed he thought of this ranch as his forever home. He loved my apple pies, and I was expected to make one each week, and it had to have a homemade crust. It made me feel good that he loved them and that I could have such a wonderful employee as well as a loyal friend. I asked myself, *How could God have blessed me so much?* I had had the best parents anyone could have, for they were honest and loving and guided me throughout my life with their wisdom. My sister, Mary, taught me many things, and I learned what being and having a sister really meant. Although we tested each other at times, we were not whole without each other.

With Brett getting married soon, I suggested we have the wedding at the ranch. I would meet his intended wife and, if she had not made any plans yet, we could discuss all the particulars. It was time there was some good old fun and laughter around the ranch.

Amelia was a beautiful woman and we wondered how Brett met her. Her hair was long and black like the night and blue eyes like the sparkling lake water on a fair day. She was soft spoken and we had to strain our ears to hear her speak. Her parents owned one of the clothing chains in the city. She had been educated at the university and worked in her father's shop. It was such a thrill for me to help plan their wedding. An orchestra was hired to play, and everything was strewn with party lights, white table cloths, everything festive. Mable was running around, even had the kids helping to do this and that even though we had hired a caterer, she had to make her own specialties of tiny sandwiches and cakes. The bar was filled with various spirits. Some of our wine made from the fruits of the farm was not to be matched. I had to have the orchestra play "Always," even though it brought back good and bad memories. I couldn't deny that it was the most beautiful wedding I had ever seen and another beautiful memory firmly placed in my heart.

—◊—

Mum began to stop eating despite all the coaxing we tried to give her. I called Dr. Snow in, and he warned me that her time was near. We tried to make her comfortable as the days turned into weeks until one morning Mable walked into her bedroom and found that she had died in her sleep with a smile on her face. We were thankful that she went peacefully. We called Reverend John to come, and when I saw him coming down the driveway, I knew this time he was an angel coming to collect her for heaven. He gave us all hugs as he entered her bedroom. Prayers were given her for a heavenly descent onto the other side of the Veil and prayers to us for the peace we would find in her death.

The reverend asked to speak privately with Mary and me, and everyone else left.

"The last time I was here, your mother asked me to do something for her at her death. It is one of my duties to ascertain that one's last wish be honored. She was very adamant that I do this for her. She wanted to let you and Mary know something that she was afraid to tell you, afraid to tell anyone. I don't know myself. She gave me a key to a locked box at the London Bank. Here it is."

He put the brass numbered key in my hand. What could Mum have been so afraid to tell us? This must be what she raved so much about forgiving her. We thought it was just a part of her illness and didn't think much about it at the time.

The coroner came and a hearse came and wheeled her away to the funeral home. It was getting late, and we were exhausted. Although we were dying to go to the bank, out of respect for Mum, we decided to wait till the funeral. We were going to lay her next to Dad, overlooking the lake where her favorite wildflowers grew in the family cemetery.

Lots of friends and church members attended her funeral, and it was a beautiful service with all of Mum's favorite flowers. We all clung together, knowing that she would be missed terribly. She would now be with Dad and her long lost family. What a happy reunion that would be for them.

The next day Mary and I went to the bank with the key to the safe deposit box. Everyone there wished us their condolences. I anxiously put the key in the lock and pulled it out of its closure. Just what would we find? Slowly the key snapped and the lid came open and inside was a couple of documents. One was her will and was addressed to both Mary and me and marked "Confidential." There was a note stating to read the "Confidential" document first. My hand trembled as I grasped the envelope and opened it. It sure was Mum's handwriting.

CONFIDENTIAL

To my dear girls whom I have loved so much: I know this will come as a great shock to you. You don't know how much I have suffered over the years to keep this terrible secret. I have to explain it to you in deep detail and to let you finally know how everything came about and why I thought it had to remain a secret. Although I have been very happy with your Dad and you two, it has haunted me every day of my life. I was an orphan since a young baby. I was put on someone's doorstep wrapped in a blanket and in a basket, and there was a note stating, "Take care of my baby, I had twins and I can't take care of them both, her name is Maggie." The people whose doorstep I was put on were very sick with tuberculosis and couldn't take care of me either, so they sent me to the orphanage. An orphanage, especially during a war is a terrible place. I was bitter because my mother didn't want me and kept my sister. I got into a lot of trouble and was sent to a reform school. Finally, I was released, but I had become too old to go back to the orphanage, so I was put out on the streets. Life on the streets was even worse than the reform school; at least there I had food to eat, clothes to wear, and a bed to sleep in. I had to eat out of the garbage cans behind the restaurants and constantly had to watch my back. One day I saw your mum from the window of Mr. Dyland's shop. She looked just like me. I figured that she had to be my twin and that I had to have some family close by somewhere. If I could have been dressed in the same fine clothes she was wearing and had my hair styled like hers, we would be identical. I just needed to put on a little weight. I had a plan now to get off the streets and have a normal life. I believed that I had found my sister, and I meant to meet her.

I worked on my plan for a couple of months. I learned about her habits, her children, her husband at war, and where she lived in the country just outside the city. One day I felt like it was time to meet her. I didn't want to scare her because she probably didn't know that I existed, so I waited till the children went to their weekly visit with their aunt and caught a ride to her house. She saw me as I walked down her driveway and came outside. I stopped at the bottom of the porch steps as she came out the door. I'll never forget the look on her face when she saw me. As she descended the steps, she slipped and fell and hit her head on the stone walk way. I knew immediately that she was dead. I cried as I held her head in my hands and pressed her close to me. "What had I done?" I wanted this to be a happy time for both of us. I had finally found my twin sister. What was I going to do now? All those years of trying to find my family came rolling in my mind and now I would never have one. I felt a loss beyond sorrow, she was my twin.

I sat and held her for a long time while trying to keep the tears away and to figure out what I should do. Should I just leave? No one knew me or that I had been there. My ride dropped me off a mile down the road. I went into the house and found a blanket to wrap her in. I needed to clear my head, so I walked around the yard, behind the barn, and into the edge of the woods. There was a thick piece of metal lying on the ground, covering something up, and I figured that it was an old dug well. Then my head started thinking. Could I assume her identity? I could, after all, have that family that I had desperately longed for all my life. I wondered if I could pull it off and be a mother to her children and a wife to her husband. Would they know I wasn't their mother and he know I wasn't his wife. I knew her husband's name and knew that he was a soldier and would be coming home soon. Would he know? He had been gone for a long time, but I was willing to take that chance. I had taken chances all my life.

I knew this was a very risky thing to do, and I could be convicted if found out. I rationalized myself that if my plan worked, the children would still have a mother and their father would still have a wife. I could spare them the loss and no one would be the wiser.

I dragged her body around to the old dug well and lifted the metal covering and gently pushed her down it. It made me sick, and I had to sit down knowing what I just had done. Gradually, I got enough strength back to put the metal covering back over the opening. I went back into the house to become familiar with everything. I found her clothes closet, pulled out one of her dresses, and laid it across the bed. Tears streamed down my face as I pulled my dress over my head and threw it into the

*fireplace to burn. I had changed into one of her dresses
and had become a new person—your mother.*

*You know the rest. I have tried to be a good mother.
I loved all of you so much. Your father thought I was different, but he thought it was because we had been apart
for so long, and we hadn't been married very long before
he enlisted in the military. Gradually things changed
beyond my wildest expectations and I had that family
and all the blessings that came with it. I never believed
I could ever have what had dropped in my lap. I thank
you, all three, for saving my life. Now go and find your
real mother and give her a proper burial. I know it's too
much to ask, even in death, to forgive me.*

*Maggie is my real first name but the orphanage gave
me my last name, Smith*

THE LAST WILL OF MAGGIE SMITH

*I, Maggie Smith, being of sound mind and body, do
hereby, after all my just debts are paid, leave my entire
holdings to my nieces, Anna Elizabeth McDonald and
Mary Louise Johnson in equal shares. I respectfully request that they will continue to keep the London Soup
Kitchen open for as long as funds permit.*

Maggie Smith
The 10th day of March, 1927

Mary and I couldn't say a word. We just looked at each and fell
into each other's arms, sobbing uncontrollably. I didn't know how
long we stood there, unable to move. I felt like I needed Grayson
to cling to and help me sort this out. It was too much even for me,
and Mary was becoming too emotional. My training had to kick

in and I had to sit her down and give her all my love that a sister can possibly give another sister.

Eventually, our legs were strong enough to get us out of the bank and back at home. We called Grayson and Harvey to meet us there. With the two documents in hand, we entered the house where they were waiting. They could tell from our faces that something was upsetting us. I handed the first one for them to read. From their faces I could tell that they looked like they were reading something unbelievable. Grayson handed back the document, wrapped me in his arms, and whispered "I'm so sorry, Anna." Harvey did the same to Mary. It was a sad time for all of us. Now we understood what Mum meant when she was raving for forgiveness. It was not just from her dementia. Could she have made up all of this in her illness? We looked at the date. No, this was written long before she showed any symptoms.

We wondered if dad knew about this. Was this what he was trying to tell us when he was dying? I couldn't imagine Dad knew for he was such a Godly man. I also couldn't imagine anyone doing such a thing. She had to have been desperate for a family and a home. What a terrible life she must have been dealing with. If Maggie had run and left Mum at the bottom of the steps, we would have had to suffer the sorrow of losing her and not having a mum and Dad not having a wife.

What to do now? There was only one thing to prove this was on the up and up. We had to go back to the old home place and find that old dug well. We wondered if we should report this to the law officials. No, it might not be true so we all agreed to find out for ourselves first.

Grayson and Harvey sat us both down and gave us a little talk about being prepared for what we might find for it would be a gruesome sight if this proves out. Grayson suggested that he and Harvey should go by themselves first, but Mary and I wouldn't have it.

I remembered how to get back to the old house where we were young and growing up. As we approached the house, I could tell that it was falling down. I stood on the hill and looked back down the driveway. I could still envision Dad walking down it in his soldier's uniform and his sack thrown across his shoulder. I could see him as he got closer that he ran faster and faster as he could go with his limp to greet Mum and us. What a joyous occasion that was for us for we had talked about this day to come many times and we wondered what it would be like to have a father in our lives. Mum had cooked up apple pies, greens, and cornbread, and we all were in heaven being together as a family at last. Now as I think what would it have been like if Maggie hadn't done what she did? We would have been without a mum and Dad would have been without a wife. Was she that selfish street person who just wanted a home and family? She did break the law with disposing of Mum's body. All we know was that she could have pushed Mum down the steps. Could she have been so bitter because their mum chose to keep Mum instead of her? Could they have argued? This wouldn't have happened at all if Maggie hadn't shown up. Lots of questions, but there would never be any other answers than what we already had.

There were so many memories around this old farm place, and I wondered if anyone else had lived here after we moved. Part of the old barn where we played was still standing. I saw a lone horse out in the pasture, probably got out of the fence from the neighboring farm. Down at the end of the driveway was a big culvert where the creek flowed through when it rained. We would get in it and listen to the sound of cars running over it and shout to hear our echoes.

Grayson and Harvey made Mary and me wait till they found the dug well. The thick grass and bushes covered the lot where Mum milked the cow and where the well was. They had brought a bush axe to cut through to make a path. They could not hold us back, and as soon as a small path was made, we were right there.

Anticipation was high as to what we were sure we would find. We knew it wasn't going to be a good thing to find our birth mother's remains lying deep in an old dug well, and we clung to each other for some kind of comfort.

We were on it before we knew it. A big sheet of rusty metal under our feet stopped us in our tracks. It just had to be lifted up now. Mary said that we needed to say a prayer for Mum before it was raised. We all bowed our heads. Harvey asked God to give us the strength to accept what we might find and to bless our sweet mother.

I was in doubt then that we should have asked the law to be with us when we found her. A part of me wanted to believe that all this that Mum had written was just a figment of her dementia, but the only thing that would change that would be what we were about to do.

Grayson and Harvey got on each end of the heavy tin and carefully lifted it off the well opening. They motioned us to stay back as they looked down the deep, wide hole. It was dark down there, but they saw a red piece of clothing. I tried to remember if Mum had a red dress, and I remembered she did. Mary and I began to sob uncontrollably and Grayson and Harvey covered the well back up. We would have to notify the law to exhume her body for a decent burial.

We all headed back home with saddened hearts. We just couldn't believe something like this could happen. Could we forgive Mum or Maggie Smith? She had been our mother. We loved her and she loved us. What a complex situation. It would take a lot of praying and pondering over this. If we had been in her situation, would we have done the same thing? Would we, as a family, put her on trial and pick this pro and that con? Could we find it in our hearts and minds to forgive her, or would this best be left to her maker?

The next day, we all went down to the police station and gave a report of this horrible situation. We asked that it should not get out to the media. We were issued into the investigative department to talk to Sargent Kelley. His eyes brightened as we described all the particulars that we had found. A group of detectives were sent to the old farm to investigate and the next day was scheduled for the exhumation. We all wanted to be there when the body would be pulled up. Grayson and Harvey advised Mary and me not to be there, but we wouldn't have it again. Later, as I recall, we decided against it. How could we watch our Mum being pulled up like that? The vision of it would bear on our minds the rest of our lives and we probably would have nightmares.

It *was* our poor Mum. I dropped down on my knees when I heard the news. Mary was inconsolable and we clung to each other as we had never done before for as our feelings at that time were indescribable. Nothing was left to do now but give her a proper burial. Unfortunately, the news had gotten out to the press, and we had to deal with that. They couldn't even wait till she was buried. How heartless we thought that was, and now we had to bury and mourn two mums

CHAPTER 12

Another era of our lives had gone by with both Mum and Mum Maggie and Dad gone. We had ourselves now and less stress, yet we missed them terribly. The ranch was continuing to grow with more cattle and more fields being planted. Cotton was the king again, and we grew plenty of it. The fields of cotton with their fluffy bowls looked like white fields of snow. With so much demand on my time at the ranch, I decided to retire and help. We had to hire more ranch hands, and they had to be fed. Mable needed some help in the kitchen, too. Actually I was becoming a pretty good cook, too, and I liked to watch the French chef, Gloria Child, on television and imitate her voice. I had some specialty dishes I liked to make, but the guys didn't care, they would eat anything.

My house needed much cleaning since it had three stories, and I hadn't gotten to the third story and the attic since I moved here. It wasn't that bad, but it was dusty, and needed a thorough clean out. One day when Mable and I finally caught a little time, we started in the attic. The church was going to have a yard sale for the needy and I felt like there would be some things up there we could contribute. Now that the weather had cooled down, it wasn't so hot up there. So we grabbed our cleaning supplies and went up, hoping to find some empty boxes. A few cobwebs met us face to face as we embarked from the stairs. Luckily, there was electricity there, and we pulled the cord for light. Gosh, there was lots of stuff stacked all around from prior generations long ago. We began to work through the cobwebs first, so we could maneuver around to see everything. There were lots of old books, furniture, clothes, family portraits, and miscellaneous items. I was like a child in a candy store as I always liked to rummage through old things. We found old baby cribs, toys, children's christening dresses, letters, greeting cards, and old-fashioned strollers. I was hoping to find something significant about my ancestors.

We found lots of items that we could donate to the church yard sale that first day and I knew it was going to take about a week to get around to all the stuff in there. I kept hoping that I would find a treasure, perhaps heirloom jewelry or a pot of gold. There was an old desk in the corner by a dormer, with drawers full of old papers, pens, miscellaneous lapel pins, cigar humidor, old keys, and a wooden box with a lock but no key in it. We tried all the old keys, but none would open it. "Should we break it?" we asked ourselves. No, it was too nice of a box. Maybe we would find it lying around somewhere else. Curiosity killed the cat and I was no different. I wouldn't rest till I got that box open.

I had heard from the neighbors that this house was haunted, but we had seen no signs of anything strange. Of course we would hear squeaks and a few bumps with the settling of the house, but I thought that it should be settled by now as old as it is. We knew how lots of people get rumors started about old houses such as ours. They would say, "Oh, so and so died in that bedroom and they still wander around. They don't like change, so don't change anything or they will get mean and do mean things." Another said, "The attic is haunted, they used to lock their kids up there when they were bad for days, and one died. The cook died, just fell over dead in the kitchen holding an iron kettle with boiling water and it splashed in her face and the hot pot hit a baby in the head and killed it." We knew that Mr. Dyland died there, because he had a stroke. But we also knew that he would never harm or haunt anybody in life or death. Mum also died in her bedroom, but I never believed in ghosts. I had never seen one.

With all this talk of the house being haunted, I became more aware of everything around me in the house. With Mum and Dad being here and all the running of the ranch, I hadn't had much time to think about the house before. There were lots of painted portraits of the prior families of Mr. Dyland. Many were highly decorated soldiers who had fought in the war of eighteen twelve. A few were almost life size, hung over the mantles and through the house. Some were the ladies of long ago with French attire and featured hats. I knew one was his mother, and she was a beautiful woman, maybe about twenty-five at the time of posing. Her hair was high atop her head and she wore a long, flowing white gown. The artist captured the most sensitive, abject look on her face. I have yet to see a photo or portrait in that place and time with the subject smiling. I heard someone say that they had nothing to smile about and another said they had bad teeth and didn't want to show them. Whatever, I would look deep in her face and ask her what was her story, why did she look so sad.

Mable and I were on our third day in the attic. It was so dusty there that we had to wear a bandana over our faces. So far no key had turned up, and my curiosity was getting the best of me, but I didn't want to damage the box. It was an expensive-looking wood box with inlaid mother of pearl with a Chinese design. I did find another box with a pearl necklace and earrings inside and I tested the earrings to see if they were real. If you run your teeth over them, and they are slick and smooth, then they are fake. If you do the same, and they are scrunchy, then they are real. They proved to be the latter. I had studied Mrs. Dyland portrait and remembered that she wore pearls, these same pearls and earrings. I took the necklace out of the box and examined them closely. The pendant was that of an oriental design, like the lid of the wooden box with small rubies all around the edges. Maybe they were designed by the same designer. Anyway I was sure they were very expensive.

There were many old clothes. Dealing with the soup kitchen and the clothing donations, I had learned to go through the pockets. I found one sweater hanging on a coat tree that I recognized and remembered seeing Mr. Dyland wearing from time to time. I fumbled through the pockets, and bingo, there was a small key. Quickly I ran to the box and inserted it right in, and the lock snapped open. In it was a journal with the writing "Personal Journal of John Barry Dyland." I was so happy that now I could learn more about his life growing up, and I made an early appointment with my bed that night, so I could start reading it. I could tell that he skipped periods of time just like most who try to keep a journal. It had a green, worn leather cover with tattered edges and yellowed pages.

—⁘—

Grayson hadn't met Mr. Dyland. He knew that he had willed the house and land to me; Mum, his money; Dad, the shop; and paid off Mary's house and shop. I was always talking about him and telling him what a good person he was to our family. I told him what we had found in the attic and I was going to start reading his journal that night and I was so excited. Grayson was anxious, too, to hear about this man who had been so important in our lives.

I told Mable that I would like to have an early dinner, so I could retire early to start reading the journal. She was glad as she could catch up on some things at home. She had found some toys in the attic for the children and they needed to go through them to see what they wanted. I told Ted to tell the crew that the evening meal would be an hour earlier.

The journal started in the year of March 16, 1890

> *John Barry Dyland*
> *It is today that I start recording my life. I am fifteen years old, and I live with my parents, John Wesley Dyland and Margie Arlene Dyland. I attend the Romand School for Boys in Hampton, England. All I can write today is*

that I saw a beautiful girl and I intend to make her my girlfriend. She has long orange hair and blue eyes. She has a cute figure.

March 17, 1890
I found out her name today, it's Rebecca. I talked to her, and I think she likes me.

March 18, 1890
Dad and I had a quarrel about my chores. I know he's right. I will have to do better, but I can't stop thinking about Rebecca.

March 19, 1890
Dad made me stay home and do chores.

March 20, 1890
I had to go back to school. I want to see Rebecca so badly.

I scanned through the usual everyday writing to get to some of the more important events in his life. I ran upon this:

May 29, 1890
Becky and I are dating. I like to kiss her. I want more and I want her so bad.

May 30, 1890
We plan to meet late tonight in the barn. It's late, late now and Becky and I met in the barn and made love. We both had never done it before. It was all I had dreamed of. We plan to meet again soon. I love her so much.

June 16, 1890
Becky and I met again in the barn, and we made love till just before day break. I love her beautiful breasts.

July 29, 1890
I met Becky at the train station, and she tells me that she's pregnant. What will we do with a baby? We're too young, and our parents will kill us.

September 9, 1890
I told my parents and they got very angry. They plan to send me away to boarding school in America, and I'm to have no contact with her ever again.

October 3, 1890
I miss Becky so much. What will she do with our baby? What will she think of me for deserting her and not acknowledging that the baby is mine? She will think that I didn't love her and I didn't want to see her again. That would be far from the truth.

March 8, 1890
I heard that Becky had twins. I wanted to see them so badly, but father forbade it. He said that I was too young to support and care for two babies and that I should just put it out of my mind forever. He also said that they might not even be mine. I got very angry with him. How dare he say such a thing about Becky? I knew I was the father. I had no doubt.

I fast forwarded to April 5, 1895

It is bearing on my mind and I have to try and find my children.

April 30, 1896
I have tried to find Becky and my children but to no avail.

May 8, 1897
I found Becky. She is married and has one of the twins, Olivia. She wouldn't answer my question as to where the other one was till I promised her that I wouldn't have anything to do with her and Olivia now has a father that loves her as his own. What could I say? She didn't even have my name. I had to agree that he was the only father she had ever known. She said that she couldn't take care of both and put her on someone's doorstep. I was appalled. She couldn't tell me whose doorstep, but she had the address. I immediately left to find the address of the people she left her with. The house was empty. I asked the neighbor where the former residents moved. "To the cemetery; they both had tuberculosis," they said. I thought next they probably put her in an orphanage. I was so out of my mind. Why did this have to happen? I had loved my parents, but I resented them for making me denounce my children. With all the money they had, they could at least have helped with their care and support. Those were their grandchildren.

May 9, 1897
I went to the orphanage to try to find my child. Surly they kept records of the children they admitted and I had run into a brick wall again. It was during the war, and they had so many children that it was hard to do records. I told them that her first name was Maggie. After an hour, they came up with six girls named Maggie and about the same year and age. I told them that her hair was red, thinking that maybe that would help. Sure enough, one had red hair. They had given her the last

name of Smith since she came with only her first. My heart skipped a beat. "Well, where is she?" I asked. Because they were so overcrowded, she had been sent to another orphanage in Hampton.

May 12, 1897
I made my way to the orphanage in Hampton. They were even more unprepared to give me any answers. Where was my daughter? I just could not find her.

May 18, 1911
I never could get my children out of my mind. I yearned to see them and to be a father to them, but it just wasn't in the cards and never would be. Maybe one day I will find Maggie and that would be the happiest day of my life. Although I couldn't be a father to Olivia, I could watch her grow up and still be close by her. I knew it was best that she not know I was her father.

June 12, 1915
Since the death of Rebecca, I found a way to be with my daughter, Olivia. I still didn't think I should divulge the fact that she was mine. She had a father, a good man, my friend, and at this late date, she should always be his child.

October 03, 1936
Olivia has grown into a beautiful woman, and I love her so much. I never stopped searching for Maggie, and I never found her. At my age now, I feel that my time is nearing. Anna, my grandchild should own this house and farm—she is family. I hope she will find this and one day will be able to forgive me.

I didn't know if it would have been a good thing if Mr. Dyland had lived long enough for the rest of the story. Maybe it was best he didn't.

I skipped through the many pages as I read about his life. He had married, but she died young and had no children. He studied at Yale and became an attorney till he retired early and bought his first haberdasher and later two more across the city. He took care of his mother and father till their death and upon their death they willed him everything. They had amassed a fortune from old blue blood money from past generations and all had lived in this house. I thought as much as all their portraits were hung in various impromptu places in the house and all the women were wearing the pearls.

—⁂—

What a shock it would have been if Dad had known that the woman he had lived with as his wife was not his wife at all. I fear he would have never been able to accept her especially if he knew what had happened to our real Mum.

We buried Mum on the hillside overlooking the lake and on the other side of Dad in the family cemetery. It was hard to remember her as my mother since Maggie had been a mother to us. We had loved her as our mother and had all the wonderful memories of her as we grew up and into adulthood. Maybe God will eventually instill into our heart the power of forgiveness and I pray every day that Maggie will be forgiven, too.

We all had a hard time getting over this and our hearts were heavy with sadness. The media had gotten hold of it, and it was all over the broadcast news and in the newspaper. The gates to the ranch had to be doubly enforced to keep the people out. We were virtually imprisoned from reporters wanting our pictures and story. Brett had to oust one climbing over the fence and had to string barbed wire over the top.

Our solace was found within God and each other. Mary closed her shop for a couple of weeks. She stayed at the ranch, hoping that things would die down soon, for it was hard to face everyone with questions. Even seeing sympathy in their eyes was almost too much to take.

I found it hard to sleep every night, thinking about my real mum. How could we not have known the difference? Mary and I were young and all, we, as kids, thought was what all young kids think at that age. Who would have thought anything like this? They were definitely look-alikes in every way. Dad knew since he had been gone so long that she would not be the same and he would not be either. He knew that they would have to get reacquainted.

CHAPTER 13

Mum Maggie had left quite a bit of money from her inheritance. Mary and I spent lots of time figuring out what we could do to improve the shelter. Extra beds were needed, and extra tables in the dining room were needed, too. We wanted to put extra showers in and extra partitions for more privacy. The kitchen needed to be expanded, and more refrigeration was needed. I thought that a program was most important to help streeters get on their feet by working with them on job training. Some could not even read or write, so we advertised for volunteer tutors. We needed more volunteers to work on the clothes' donations, to clean and sort them. The food pantry needed more organization. Our ranch donated beef each month and eggs from our chickens. Grants and donations also helped keep the shelter open.

Things were beginning to settle down somewhat. We were able to leave the ranch, but we all wore a hat and sunshades so as not to be recognizable. It felt good just to get out and do some shopping. Mary was considering opening her shop back up, too. Although we had good people at the shelter, it still needed to be checked on. We all had agreed that at the first sign anyone wanted to talk about Mum, we would immediately cut them off. Other things were needed to be attended to rather than discussing that matter.

Everything worked out pretty good for most people were respectful and knew how we felt. Now we had some legal matters to attend to, concerning the transfer of funds and the deed of the shelter. The plans we had all worked on were soon going to be in place, and we were all going to be much better equipped to serve the growing number of people who needed us. We, too, needed them to fill our time with happy and fulfilling moments, rather than those filled with sorrow.

Several months later, I was contacted by a national publishing company to write our story. At first I was totally against it. How could we air our dirty laundry for the general public? I was totally caught off guard. Absolutely not, how dare they even think that we would do such a thing to our family. They said it would be written in a way to empathize with Mum and the readers would understand why she did what she did. It would cover mental illness, poverty, desperation, and a young life filled with rejection. It would cover the love she had for her twin, if only for a few moments, and the tragedy of losing it as soon as she found it. It would cover the torment she had to endure the rest of her life with the secret she felt she had to keep. I had to discuss it with Mary, Harvey, and Grayson.

They didn't know that was just part of our family secrets. Would we be able to tell them the other story, and that one of the richest family in London was involved? Mr. Dyland's parents were a proud family and would have done anything or paid anything to keep their name out of it. Fortunately, they had an obedient son, so they didn't have to. All in all, I knew that Mr. Dyland lived a life of desperation not being able to find his daughter and not being able to claim Olivia and Maggie as his own. What would our real mum have been like if she had been our mum as we grew into adulthood? There are some things in our lives that we have to deal with and mix them with the things that are joyous. That's just life as everyone has, and I can't think of any family that doesn't have to do this. We, as individuals, have to make life better as we journey through it and learn to see the happy side of life. Mary and I and our spouses, being the close-knit family we were, decided to do this and enjoy what God had given us. This great, big world out there had yet a lot to offer us and we intended to accept it with open arms.

We pondered and pondered the book offer and decided to go with it. It was a hard decision, but we thought maybe the story needed to be told. Within two months after publication, it made it to the best seller list, and later, it was made into a major motion picture. What could we say or feel about it only that it happened to us.

Our lives went on and we made the best of it. As we got older, as with all families, member after member began to have physical problems. Mary had blood pressure problems, and she wasn't able to keep it under control. One day she called me to come over because she didn't feel well, and as I approached her bedroom, I knew something was very wrong. She had had a major stroke and was slumped over on the floor. We buried her on the ranch close to Dad in a shady spot that she loved so well under the tulip poplar tree in the family cemetery. Harvey was devastated. He could never get over her death. He died one month later of the same condition, and I feel that he may have grieved himself to death.

I lost Grayson, my beloved, five years later in an accident. He fell down the stairs at the house, and I suspected that he had a stroke. I tried to keep my chin up and just be thankful for what I had, the family I had, and the memories of my life. I miss being close to him at night when we retired to bed as that was our time to discuss our plans for the next day and whatever else we wanted and needed to discuss. The most important was the intimacy we shared with one another; the sweet, loving relationship; and our conversations that always ended with, "I'm so glad you're my wife," and "I'm so glad you're my husband."

—◊◊—

I took the pearls and ruby pendant that grandmother Dyland wore in her portrait to the jeweler to be cleaned. He called and told me that it was ready and he needed to talk to me when I came to pick it up. I thought maybe it needed some extended repair work or maybe some of the gems needed to be replaced. But I had never noticed any of those missing. When I arrived, he brought it out and told me that he discovered something unusual. The pendant had a hidden compartment that could be turned in a certain way to open. He turned it for me, revealing a small, folded piece of paper with a series of numbers on it. The numbers looked like some kind of code to a combination locker trunk or a safe maybe. I had never seen a safe, but I hadn't completely gone through the attic. Now, I was like a person with a plan. I raced back to the house in anticipation of searching for a safe or something that had a lock.

I had plenty of time on my hands. I had felt before that this big, old mansion still had more secrets to give up than what I had found in just two attic visits. The vastness of the house, attic, and basement still amazed me, and I was always a curious person who liked to plunder in unexplored areas. I knew there was lots of family history to discover and I was ready to do it.

It was still early in the morning in the attic, and the sun was streaming through the dormers. It was brighter than when Mary and I were in there, and I could see to the farther end. First I spotted several large trunks that I was hoping weren't locked, but the numbers looked more like a combination to a safe, so I looked father beyond them. Things were stacked on top of each other almost to the ceiling in some spots. The dust was getting to me, and I was glad that I had brought my bandana to cover my nose and mouth. I moved item after item, old lamps, pots, picture frames, hat boxes, etc. Finally, in a far corner, I spotted a sectioned off partition and raced toward it, stumbling over boxes as my excitement grew stronger. As I approached it, I noticed that it had a lock on it, too, and it presented another challenge for me. This ancient house was not about to give up any more secrets very easily.

We had guessed that four generations of the Dyland family had lived in the house. Gathering from old letters and portraits hanging on the wall, they all had never lived anywhere else. John Barry Dyland, I can now call him my grandfather, did not have any siblings that we knew of and I was sad that the Dyland name was stopping here. His father, John Wesley, was an investment banker. I figured that was one factor in my grandfather choosing to go into the banking business. It still seems odd to call him my grandfather and I wished that I, as a child and as an adult, had known him as a grandfather. I had never known a grandmother or a grandfather. I think every child needs to experience the love that both can give. I missed having them, to hug them, and to sit in their laps, and feel that special bond. I knew he thought he was doing the best thing by not claiming my mom as his daughter, because he felt like he would be interrupting their marriage, and she already had a wonderful stepdad who treated her as his own.

So now, I was at a standstill as to where to look for more keys to unlock the closet that I believed held the safe. I refused to let this deter me from plundering deeper in the attic. I was getting farther away from the light-filtering dormers, so I had to go back downstairs to find a flashlight. I would be more prepared in the future to always carry extra means of light. I had planned to spend all day searching for a safe and anything I could find out about my newly discovered and long-lost family. As the day wore on and darkness began to creep in, I couldn't help think about the rumors of this house being haunted. I hadn't seen or heard anything in the years living here before. Nevertheless, every bump and creak I heard brought my attention and awareness that I was alone here. I ran into a large wooden box and knocked it down. Immediately I thought that someone was in front of me. Silly me, it was just a dress form, used in dressmaking. Lots of people believe in spirits, but I don't, and I never will. I'll have to see one to change my thinking. It's all in the minds of weak people, I thought.

I pushed on forward, stepping on and over boxes and furniture. Suddenly I lost my balance and fell over a box. Music began to play like old music from an old phonograph. Right in front of me falling toward me popped up a woman with straggly gray hair. Her face was distorted and cracked and her mouth was all blistered looking. My mind was rethinking that ghost thing right about then. I ran as fast as I could, stumbling over everything on my way to the door and downstairs. As I entered the kitchen, I sat down trying to get my breath. After a few minutes, I took stock of what had just happened and realized that I had overreacted. That woman was not a ghost but was a very old manikin that probably was in Mr. Dyland's shop at one time. As far as the music, that's for another day, I had had enough excitement for one day.

—⁕—

It was two more days before I returned to the attic. I had been busy searching the house for anything that might have been written in any journal or on any tidbits of paper anywhere referring to anything about a safe. I realized that this house would take some time to rummage through for there are six bedrooms on the first floor, not to mention the extra rooms for various purposes. Some of them looked like they had been left the same as when each family member left them. There are six bedrooms on the second floor and four bedrooms on the third floor. There is a large balcony from the third floor where one can sit for fresh air or drink their hot tea. Downstairs consists of a forty-foot entry hallway, leading to a huge gathering room with winding stairways descending on two sides. The dining room is off to one side and consists of a long table that can seat twenty-four easily. It leads to the servants pantry and then to the kitchen. Next to the kitchen are the servants' quarters, consisting of two bedrooms. On one side of the dining, the library leads into the parlor and then to the music room. On the other side of the dining room are the gentlemen's office and then the sunroom and sewing room.

I found a lot of old keys of all different shapes and sizes. I thought to myself that this house is a house to be reckoned with.

There might even be secret rooms that I hadn't discovered, as I had seen in movies where some old houses had them off from the library and there would be a certain book you could move and a door to a room would automatically open. I moved a lot of books but none opened a door. Maybe if Mr. Dyland knew, there might be something about it in his diary, maybe in the back of it. I had just scanned through it before and hadn't read it completely. I made a date with myself that night to search through it again. I learned a lot more about him though, but nothing about a safe. I'm betting that he didn't know that a safe even existed. And I thought about his mother, my great grandmother? Did she know? I wondered. Which generation put it there?

The next thing I thought to do was to try to find the family Bible for the information about most births, deaths, weddings, and other things about the family were usually recorded there. I was anxious to find out, too, all I could about my too long-lost relatives. As I began my Bible search, I got the worst feeling of being alone than I had ever had. I missed everybody so terribly. Loneliness can be a vessel of defeat. I had to look at myself in the dresser mirror to remind me that I couldn't go there. Mary had been by my side in almost all our lives. She was the soft, kind person that I always wanted to be like. I missed her tender heart and her quick humor in the silly things we did together. She was a part of me and I missed not being a mother and protector of a child which I failed to be a protector of. Yes I, too, shared part of the guilt of my lost child which Johann paid the ultimate price for. Yes, everyone was gone but me, and I knew that my life was going in the wrong direction. I had to do something about it. I just couldn't sit in this house day in and day out no matter how many mysteries this ancient house held and was begging to be found out, but that adventure in me overrode and dominated my every thought.

I had my work cut out for me, and I would find out this mystery sooner or later or get a carpenter to come and tear the closed in corner down for me. Right then, I was going to try the keys I had found in various places. Since I figured out the ghost situation, I was not afraid to start my search again. I had opened every lid and drawer downstairs that I could find, but to no avail. Did my grandfather, I wondered, ever plunder in the attic and basement? Did he even know that there was a safe? I didn't even know for sure myself, but that code was for something that my grandmother had valued and wanted to keep secret? But did she even know that there was a secret compartment in the necklace? Did any of them know it was there except the one who put it there? I got to thinking. Did any one of them know? Could it have been placed there by the gift bearer, perhaps their husband or admirer? Every lady of the house had worn it in their portrait that hung on the walls, and I wondered which one had placed it there. The paper the code was written on was very old, thin and yellowed. I would probably had never known myself if the jeweler had not found it. My excitement was mounting. The safe might not even be inside that corner closet but my bloody curiosity wouldn't let me stop till I found out.

I had a lot of questions about my Dyland family. How did they amass such wealth? Where did they come from? My curiosity was at high ebb, and now I had time to search for the answers. In the years before, I was so consumed by my career, the duties I had running the ranch and taking care of Mum that my time was all taken up. I needed to do this, too, to fill my time alone and to satisfy my mind as to what background my family had.

Climbing those stairs was getting to be strenuous for me, but I trekked up them with renewed adrenal. First, I wanted to solve the puzzle of the music and where it was coming from. I had passed several pipe organs on my way to the corner, but I knew they wouldn't just start playing anything. I had recognized the tune "Blue Danube" and figured that it came from a music box. Since I stumbled over a lot of things, one could just have started playing. Sure enough, I reached the spot and saw a box spilling music boxes. Someone in the family must have collected them. I looked beyond them and saw the twisted manikin lying on the attic floor. She looked like she had been there locked up in her dark, dusty haven as if she had to watch over all the stored treasures for her masters for generations. Apparently when she fell, her head cracked open. I had a feeling of sorrow knowing that she had been here for such a long time and I was the cause of her broken head. I shined the light on her to see if maybe I could repair her. What did I see? Deep in the crevice of her nose was a tattered pull string silk bag. My hands were shaking and my fingers were nimble as I pulled apart the string that was gathered tight. Several keys fell out in my hand and I was so excited, now, hopefully one would fit the lock and I asked myself, what were the chances of ever finding them. Now I had to find out which key would.

The corner enclosure was made of thick metal, and if I would have had to have it torn down, it would have been a major job. Whoever built it was hiding something and went to major extremes to hide it. I finally made it to the end of the attic and pulled out the keys from the draw string bag. I tried one. It didn't work. I tried the second one, and as soon as it touched the key hole, it immediately opened. Cobwebs and dust met me as I stepped inside. I reached with my arms and hands to brush back the long and thick cobwebs and pulled my bandana tighter to my face. I saw nothing but empty space in no more than about a nine-by-twelve room. As I stepped farther and closer to the middle, I noticed that the floor felt different under my feet. I heard a few squeaks as I took a couple steps farther, it didn't feel as solid. Maybe underneath it was hollow. I shined my flashlight down to get a better look. Some of the edges of the planks seemed to be worn more than others. *There must be something underneath.* I thought. How was I going to get those floor boards up by myself? I could get someone to help me, but whoever went to these measures to conceal whatever must have hidden something only he knew about. No, I didn't want anyone else to know about this and I was going to try anything by myself to find out.

I had to go back down and out to the tool shed to find something that I could use to pry up the floor boards and found a crowbar hanging on the wall. I thought that would do it. My flashlight wasn't going to be enough, so I found a lantern and filled it with oil. My excitement was mounting, and I wanted to be prepared for what I might find, for it could be skeletons. Maybe one of my forefathers was a murderer. I didn't know but I was about to find out.

I stopped off in the kitchen to get a drink and pray that God's spirit would be with me as I knew this old house was finally going to give up one of its fast-held secrets of long ago. Which one of my forefathers built this mansion? I felt in my bones that the first Dyland who built this house held all the answers. I was going to try to find out tonight from the family Bible.

I went back up the stairs, having to stop and rest a little till I got to the attic again. I had made a pretty good path from my trips before and could navigate better. Finally there, I stooped down to pry the boards up, and, to my surprise, they came up easily. There was a stairway leading down to another room. *How could this be?* I thought. It would have to have gone down to the bedroom below? I lowered myself down the stairs, but there was no bedroom. It would have to have been partitioned off from the bedroom below. There was another closet with a lock. I inserted the second key in the lock, and it opened. There it stood, about a six-foot iron safe covered in dust and cobwebs. I quickly swept away the cobwebs around the lock and took out the yellowed slip of paper with the numbers. As I punched the last number in, the loud click sounded deafening to my sensitive ears. I immediately froze and the realization of a booby trap threw me to caution. I had to straighten up, get my breath, and think. Should I throw caution to the wind and go ahead and just open it? Ummm! To do or not to do was the question? How could I open it without being in direct contact with it? I decided that I needed to sleep on this, but I knew that sleep was not to be for me that night.

I was right; sleep did not come to me because I was too uptight to settle down. I thought and thought about how to open the safe door without being directly in the front of it. Maybe I could get a ladder and crawl to the top from behind with some stiff wire with a hook on it. I could hook the handle and pull it upward. Yes, maybe that would work. I would not be directly in front of it if anything dangerous popped out of it when it opened. That was the only way I thought would work. I planned to try it in the early morning. I can't describe how excited I was but yet so bloody apprehensive.

After I had finally made a decision, I was totally exhausted and fell asleep for an hour or so. The sun streaming through my window felt warm on my face and I woke groggy as hell, but it did not deter me from my plan that day. Luckily, I had seen a ladder in the attic, and I knew that it was going to be hard to get up and down the stairs, but there was that renewed adrenal to help me. Maybe there was an easier way to get to it. I went and inspected the bedroom. I figured that it descended down into it and knew that it probably would be plastered up. All the walls seemed to be normal, but I wasn't satisfied with just looking at them. I took a pole and began knocking to see if some spots would have a hollow sound or maybe a closet would have a hidden compartment, but I didn't have any luck with that, so I proceeded with my original plan.

It was hard, but I took my time and made it up to the attic and to the room with the stairs going down to the room with the safe. I sure felt the effects of my aging and had to rest again before I put my plan in place. After I rested a bit, I moved the ladder to the back of the safe and climbed to the top with the wire with which I had made a hook on the end. It took me about ten tries to hook the handle, but I finally did it. I was sweating and shaking and held my breath as I slowly pulled it upward. The safe door opened and nothing happened—no dynamite igniting and no evil-looking stuff coming out of it. I was hoping that I wouldn't have an evil spell cast on me. I let my breath out. At last my curiosity would be satisfied and one of the secrets of the house would finally be revealed.

I climbed down the ladder, trying to be careful, and moved cautiously to the front of the safe. I can't tell you what I saw. I was so astounded! The safe's shelves were full of gold bullion. *Was this real?* I asked myself. Who put it there? How long ago? Where did it come from? I looked at some of the yellowed, cloth sacks holding different treasures, with the name Bank of--, but the last name had been cut out. This sent a message to me that one of my forefathers was a thief, and this is where all the money came from. I assumed that he had so much that this was just some that he hadn't cashed in before he died. I was so amazed for I had never envisioned such wealth.

—m—

Now more than ever, I had to get busy in the library and try to find out more about this family that I descended from. I'm assuming the thief was the one who built this mansion. Portraits of my forefathers hung on the tall walls throughout the house. It was up to me to determine which one was the eldest. My first thought was to go back to that old family Bible. Some in the portraits were dressed in military uniforms and some were dressed in fine clothing of the era, the very finest. All the women were adorned with rubies, diamonds, and pearls. The men had large rings of gold and different forms of precious gems.

The next morning I took my pen and paper to the family cemetery to try to find the oldest tombstone. It was in a beautiful spot overlooking the lake and had always been taken care of. The landscaping was just breathtakingly beautiful with perfectly shaped shrubs and lilies of all varieties among the rows of scented roses of every color. All the tombstones were tall and made of marble. They were finely carved with flowers and designs fittingly of the person buried. Some had ships, horses, pets, and military insignias. I was amazed at the number of children's graves, mostly babies at a very young age, some at just one day old. It made me very sad as I copied all the names and dates.

—⚬—

It didn't dawn on me at the time that this all might be mine, and that I might be the richest woman in the world. I thought I was already rich enough with all I had inherited and what I had acquired from my career and the ranch. How much more could I ever hope to spend in my lifetime? I was overcome with a feeling of extreme thankfulness. Life was good and beautiful.

My thoughts were that this gold had been stolen from some bank somewhere. Since the bank's name was cut out of the cloth bags, I didn't know the name of the bank. Unless I could find something else with a bank name on it in the safe, I probably would never know. I also knew that I must not tell anyone about what I had discovered; no, not a soul.

I settled down in my bedroom that night with the family Bible and various photo albums trying to match up names, dates, and photos to the names I had copied from the cemetery. Joseph Allen Dyland, came to my attention, born in Ireland in 1769. I scanned over the pages. The next generation of Dylands was John Paul Dyland, born here in London in 1799. My great-great grandfather, John Wesley, was born in 1840. My grandfather, John Barry Dyland, was born in 1875. I matched the dates and names from the photos and the Bible of births. I assumed that all had deceased and the lineage stopped with me.

I had lots to think about and I spent the next two weeks trying to figure out things. Questions and more questions were on my mind. I didn't know how the heck I was going to get any answers.

First question was: Where did it come from? Had the gold been a collection by one of my forefathers, I do not understand why would the name of the bank be cut out of the bags? How could he have acquired so much wealth? Second question was: Which forefather put it there? He went to extreme measures to keep it hidden. I would have thought that it would have been the first one or eldest one, Joseph Allen, since he had probably been the one who built this house. Third question was: Was he alone in committing this crime? It would have taken a lot of thought and planning to pull off such a heist. It would have taken more than one person just to haul all that gold out. Fourth question was: How was I going to find out anything? I wondered how long it had been hidden in its dark tomb, just waiting for a ray of light to shine its brilliant color again. Fifth question was: Is this gold legally mine? It's in my house and everyone from that period of time is dead. Sixth question was: How much is all this worth?

I went back to the safe, hoping to find a note or anything else in the safe. I thought maybe I should look at the date on the manufacturing and serial number label of the safe. It couldn't have been before the safe was manufactured. I finally found it on the inside of the door and it read 1754, Dublin. Ireland. So, of course it had to have been after 1754.

I started working on the fourth question. Joseph had been born in Ireland in 1769. I presumed that this bank heist might have occurred there and he hi-tailed out of there afterward and settled here in London. He would have had the means to build this estate and enough money to last for generations to come and obviously more.

I thought maybe I could find about any big bank heist in archived newspapers of Dublin, Ireland. It was not known if they even archived them in that era of time. It was only 363 miles and I intended to make the trip to satisfy my curiosity. I called my driver and set the trip for the next day. It had been a long time since I had been to Ireland, and I reveled in its fresh green hills and lush valleys. A trip anywhere was just what I needed to get out of the house and enjoy the countryside. My head kept going over everything that had happened in the last week. What are the odds of anyone finding what I found in my attic in theirs? I would think none to zero. If I did find out about a major bank heist in that time frame, would I have the balls to give it back? Could I disgrace the Dyland name and ever be able to hold my head up again? What a question I asked myself? As far as I knew, the robbery might have been made somewhere else, but where?

We drove to the Library of Ireland where archived newspapers were kept. I spent all day going through different years. There were several articles on bank robberies, but the take wasn't near as much as those gold bars were worth. I would go back home and look in London's archive.

The next day I was so uptight wondering about everything that I decided to give it a break and just lounge around all day. The images of all that wealth kept flashing in my mind. How could I cash those gold bars without someone getting suspicious? If I just did one occasionally, maybe no one would even suspect. They would just think that it was from a collection. I put it out of my mind and spent the rest of the day reading a good book.

CHAPTER 14

I went shopping the next day in Mary's old shop. I didn't know why, I had more clothes than I would ever wear and many I had never worn. The house, although as big as it was, was beginning to close in on me, and I needed some fresh surroundings. The new owners had made a lot of changes and the new styles amazed me, but I could still feel Mary's presence here. She loved this shop and all the customers that came in. All those customers were sure to keep on returning. She had that air about her with her smile and gentle words and genuine love for everyone.

I purchased a few items and was going down the street to the drugstore when I heard someone call my name.

"Dr. Anna," he said.

I turned around and it was one of my old patients.

"Charles," I replied. "It's so nice seeing you again! How long has it been? How are you?"

"I'm fine, and you?" he asked.

We walked a while and then sat down on a park bench, each with an ice cream cone. Charles Roberts had been my patient for two years, and I knew him to be a caring, soft-hearted man who had been dealt a hard life. I would like to think that I helped him get his life back in order. He was a nice-looking man and was about my age. He now looked like a successful businessman—clean cut, and wearing the best of clothes. His statue was lean, and his gait was that of a proud man. We talked about old times and what had been going on in both our lives since we last saw each other.

He had lost his wife five years before. I had not even talked to another man like this since Grayson, and had not even thought about another man. I was beginning to get self-conscious about my hair and nails. I hadn't been to a salon since Grayson. Was I beginning to feel an attraction for this man? I was beginning to get a hint of chocolate in my mouth.

The next morning he called and asked me to have dinner with him that night. We met at the Palisades Restaurant on Fourth Street. We really enjoyed the meal and champagne and talked till we thought we might get kicked out. Since my driver dropped me off, he offered to drive me home. I no sooner got the door open than he took me in his arms. I just melted as I yielded to his advances. It had been so long since I felt that warm, sexual feeling flooding my very being, and he wasn't my patient anymore. He wasn't gentle with his actions and I wasn't either. It had been too long and our sexual demands were at their highest. We both ripped each other's clothes off like wild predators. He was stiff and long and I was moist and ready as I spread my legs to accommodate him. His kisses were hot and our frantic bodies moved in rhythm to each other. I had almost forgotten how it felt to be with a man. My sexual awakening was at its peak. Each thrust brought more pleasure to both of us until we both exploded in that moment of total ecstasy. We lay back in each other's arms with gentle kisses, and we knew that this would happen again soon, very soon.

I woke up when the rain outside my window was making a soft pattering sound. I looked over on the other side of the bed. It seemed weird with a man lying there. Charles was still asleep peacefully. I thought about last night and our wild lovemaking. I had no idea how sexually starved I had been, but I didn't think I would be again. He was a good man and I was a lonely woman.

We spent the day together, riding horses after the rain ceased. The creek and lake seemed to be refreshed as well as the air. I genuinely liked this handsome man, and I felt like he liked me. We got back to the house and had a light meal. Then he had to leave, but not before we made love again. It was different from last night—slow and gentle. We took our time loving each other. He was a buyer for a local manufacturing firm and had to go out of town. I was sad to see him go, but he promised to call when he returned.

I made an appointment with the salon for my hair and nails and planned to buy some of the new styles of clothes. I was a woman and needed to do those things that a woman does to keep her femininity. I hadn't cared much lately since I hardly went anywhere or saw anybody. Charles changed all of that, and I felt young again. I looked at my body in the full-length mirror. *Not bad for my age.* I thought. He was gone all week and I counted the hours till he returned.

On the other hand, I knew I had blown caution to the wind. I was a very rich woman and could easily be taken in, so vulnerable being alone for so long. I had to think on this and not get caught up with someone who was after my wealth. In my heart I felt like this was not the case, but I had to be careful.

—∿—

I was back, trying to solve the questions of the stash of gold. I spent most of the day and night in the library, looking through old journals and photo albums. I stopped now and then, remembering the night before and the woman that I had been—the woman I didn't recognize. That stirring in me had awakened a part of me that was long denied as being me. I had a new energy abounding with a joy deep inside me that had been lost. But what should I do with this newfound embodiment of sexual release? Should I continue to let it be or should I continue to let it thrive with an appetite of rich endurance? I found myself floating as if the world was at my feet and I had wings to fly like the strong wind that came in with it.

CHAPTER 15

I took a break and filled my cup with coffee, cream, and two sugars. It was funny how the steam rose from the cup as I poured it, melting the sugar and causing the cream to swirl around in all directions. I thought my life was like that, swirling around in all directions and not knowing which way to go. Somehow the sweetness had melted away. My life had been at a standstill, and now it had offered me a way to soar like the blue birds outside on the rose of Sharon bush. I had to choose, but I was afraid to make the decisions that, I thought, would maybe alter my life.

It was exciting going through all the photo albums and seeing the different hair styles and clothing they wore. The strangers who were my family seemed to have gone through many phrases, tragedies, and many good times. There were pictures of trips they took to the United States and even to Africa. They had the means to do anything they wanted to do, and now, because I shared the same Dyland name, I had such means also. Never in my wildest dreams did I know I would be an heir of the most astute and richest family in England. I never understood how Mr. Dyland could come in the shop, knowing that Mum was his daughter and never claim her as his own. Did he think that would put a black mark on the Dyland name? Or, was he a man of his word and kept his word to Becky?

Discovering the gold was either good or bad. It would be a good thing if it was wealth accumulated from honest dealings. However, if it was there from thievery, it put a damper and a black mark on the Dyland name. Would I ever be able to discover who got it there and how? I would have gladly given it back if I only knew. Being the kind of woman I am, I could never spend any of that gold unless it was deemed legally mine to claim. For right then, this would be my secret and my secret alone.

In my observance, most of my family had been in banking and others had been attorneys. There were lots of books about law and banking. It seems kind of fitting that between them both they could easily have laundered those gold bars without anyone knowing.

I planned the next day to go to the London Library to search out the archived newspapers. It, too, was to no avail since the library had been bombed during the war and everything had been destroyed. I was at a dead end and didn't know what else I could do, but I just knew secrecy was very important and somehow time would eventually take care of everything.

Over the next few days, I thought that I needed to talk privately to Judge Roberts and I made an appointment for the next week. In the meantime it was time for Charles to come home, and I was thrilled beyond words. I wanted to tell him about the treasure I found but that still, small voice told me not to tell a soul, not even the judge. Would she want to know what the treasure was? Or, could I tell her without mentioning "gold"? Over and over I thought in my mind about how I could explain to her the situation, hoping that it would work.

I met Charles at the train station among a crowd of arriving passengers. I felt like a school girl as I saw him stepping down with his luggage in hand and looking above their heads for me. As he spotted me, a broad smile crossed his face, and I knew he was as happy to see me as I was to see him. He held me as if I had been lost for a long time and he had finally found me. We went to a small coffee shop for a sandwich and to catch up on everything. I couldn't tell him everything my week had been composed of. He asked me for a date the next night, and I gladly accepted. I offered to cook us dinner at the ranch. Charles was easy to talk to unlike how he was when I was his therapist. I still felt weird dating him, but the years had changed that code of ethics. Maybe it was something else nagging at me in the back of my mind. Could he still have some of those deep-seated emotional problems that had required therapy in the first place?

I cooked my special dish of spaghetti with my secret sauce and selected the best vintage wine from the wine cellar. Afterward, we sat in front of the fireplace and made small talk about what was happening in the world. The wine flowed down my throat, making me feel warm and desirable. I snuggled closer to Charles, knowing what the evening would bring.

—⟁—

It was time for my appointment with Judge Roberts, and I was so nervous. Everything had gone through my mind. What if I accidently told her exactly what was in the safe and she told someone and it got out to the press. Would I be at risk of being burglarized? Would I be too scared to live here anymore? The Dyland name would be disgraced for sure and in all the newspapers. This was a delicate decision to make, and I was thinking twice about it. On the other hand, I could never claim it without some legalization.

I started to cancel our appointment but I wanted to get this thing settled as fast as I could. It was weighing heavy on my mind. I wanted to get to some point of closure and knew that the puzzle of it may never be solved. I may just have to let it be and accept it.

The entrance to Judge Roberts's office smelled just like an old court house smells—paper and a little bit like mildew. Her desk was right in the middle of a wall with certificates of her law degree, her judgeship, and various other certificates of accomplishments. There were also portraits of previous judges and their expressions of staunch authority staring back at me. Sitting on her desk were small framed photos of her family and a unique paperweight that immediately caught my eye. I realized that it was her surname Coat of Arms. She glanced up at me with a look that told me she was busy and what problem could I possibly have that I had to take up her time with.

"So what brings you here, Mrs. Wilson?"

She had no idea that I had remarried after Johann.

"I have a sort of situation that I need to discuss with you," I said. "I inherited the Dyland mansion and I discovered something hidden and very valuable that I think may have been gotten by ill means."

"Yes, and I understand you inherited everything in the house, too?"

"Yes, your magistrate," I replied.

"I'm not going to ask what it is you are referring to but if you inherited the house and contents, and then it's yours to do with what you want to. The Dyland family has been an old and very respectful family. I can't even think anything in that house would have been stolen. Even so if there was anything stolen, everyone is dead by now and the statute of limitations has expired. I wouldn't be surprised that there are many valuables hidden there. If it would make you feel better, I will draw up a legal proclamation stating that any valuables found in the house is legally your property. I would like to thank you and your mom for what you have done with the soup kitchen. Now go home and don't worry, just be thankful that you had the good luck to find it," she replied.

I left out of her office letting out a breath of pent up air and so much relieved that I felt like a new person. The question now was: What was I going to do with it? I could open up a Swiss Bank account, but it was mine, and I didn't have to hide it. There was no doubt in my mind then that I was the richest woman in the world. It may sound like a grand title, but it also brings problems. I had to handle this "grand title "with kid gloves. First, I couldn't let it out that I was the richest woman and I'd have to hire body guards and put up electric fences around the house. I'd think every man who smiled at me was after my money and any woman who befriended me was the same. I could just leave it where it was and where it's been for umpteen years. Probably no one would, even after my death, ever find it. I just didn't need it and all the problems that came with it.

—⧖—

I had decided to get on with my life and focused on other things. I still had an interest in the soup kitchen and I dropped by there from time to time to see that things were as they should be. There always seemed to be more and more coming to get a bowl of hot soup and a cot to sleep on. As I watched them come in the door cold and hungry and as they eagerly devoured the hot substance, I felt so guilty that I had so much and they had so little. I took a little comfort in that I almost totally supported this kitchen. If I could have taken them all home with me, I would have, but there were just too many. I knew most of them by name and they knew mine. We all were always glad to see each other. There was one man in particular, Frank, who seemed so lost. I found myself paying attention to his ramblings. He was about fortyish and looked to be in good health. I could use another yard man to help keep the grounds at home and maybe he would be a good worker. It was always a question since some were mentally ill and could not manage a job, but I offered him one anyway and if there was one, we could work on it. To my surprise, he jumped at the idea of working outside in a beautiful garden. I learned later that he had a phobia of being inside and that's why he preferred to live outside on the streets. I always wondered why he took his food outside on the tables to eat, no matter how cold it was.

—⧖—

Charles and I were still seeing each other occasionally, but I wasn't going to let myself get too involved with a former patient of mine. I knew how mental health, especially his, worked on people. I knew from the start that we shouldn't have gotten involved. Although he seemed to be able to function and have a great career, it could always raise its ugly head from time to time. I did enjoy his company and the sex, but I could recognize a red flag from time to time. Eventually, I knew I would have to end it.

CHAPTER 16

Trying to find more about my forefathers was becoming an obsession for me, and I poured myself for hours in the scrap books, photo albums, and journals. The basement was like an unexplored playground for me that I was just waiting to play on. What would I find down there?

As I was looking through the photo albums, there were the children, some babies, some older. One picture specifically caught my attention. There was a young couple in the picture, holding a baby, and they had this saddest look on their face. I had begun to try to match names and dates from the tombstones to the same in the albums, Bible, and photos. Apparently this photo was taken just after the baby had died and they wanted this one last picture. So many babies were stillborn and many mothers died in childbirth. I could empathize with them for losing a child. It's like your heart is tearing from your body and there's nothing you can do about it, and the agony never stops.

The world was still revolving, and I found things to do other than research the family history. I had to take a break again from all the questions this house held for me. Paris was where I had always wanted to go. The romantic atmosphere heralded by lovers intrigued me. As a child I had dreamed about going there and visiting the many fashion shows, the museums, Eiffel Tower, the Palace of Versailles, and the many sidewalk cafes. Going alone would be weird, but I had almost gotten accustomed with being alone.

I had booked the three-hour train trip on the Simplon-Orient Express to Paris and decided to go on to Venice via the Simplon Tunnel through the Alps. The vision of a train ride to Paris was reputed as being for lovers. A lover I did not have since I had ended it with Charles, but I intended to enjoy myself anyway. The sights would be incredible and the cuisine and shopping would be just what I needed.

I had three days to pack, but as before on our trip to New York, I didn't pack much. My luggage needed to be able to accommodate the treasures I intended to bring back. Excitement kept me from sleeping much of the night before, but I managed to arise in time to make it to the train station. There were all sorts of people of different nationalities boarding the train. Their style of dress and hairdos stood out from the crowd. Their conversation with each other sent a little apprehension through my being, since I wasn't as affluent in the French language as I would have liked to have been. Several men offered to help me with my carry-on luggage, but I declined graciously.

The interior of the train looked nice with the fringed curtains and shades. The seats were soft yet firm enough to be comfortable. I knew I would have to sit by someone and hoped that someone would not be irritating or would need a bath. I settled down getting in the window seat so I could see the countryside and enjoy the warm sun streaming through.

The crowd was still climbing onto the train and I watched for whoever was going to sit beside me when a tall man, about fifty-ish, with a mustache tipped his hat at me. I shouldn't have had to worry, for he was clean cut and smelled of spice.

"Pardon me ma'am, I'm Tom, and I believe this is where I sit."

"Sure," I said.

We sat quietly till all the passengers were boarded and the train started rumbling and beginning its path to Paris. We made small talk for a while, finding out where we were from and about our families. Small talk it was, for I didn't like to get too familiar with strange men.

I had brought some reading material from the library to read, but the beautiful scenery rivaled the most interesting book. The trees were so green and the limbs cascaded from their trunks as if they had been measured to grow perfectly. The grass along the track was lush and green with tiny wild flowers peeking their heads out as if to say peek-a-boo. In the far distance, I could see the valleys with wildlife wandering so nonchalantly. It amazed me so much when we crossed the bridges and the water of the rivers rippled in the wind like sparkling diamonds.

I didn't know what to expect when I got to Paris. I was traveling alone for the first time, but I was sure that I could find my way. Still I was a woman traveling alone, and I knew I had to be careful. The Simplon Tunnel was coming up, and I was so excited. Hearing the rumbling, bumping change of the sound as the train descended into the tunnel gave me a start and I was afraid that I almost jumped out of my seat. Tom offered his hand to steady me as I embarrassed myself and settled back down. He seemed like a nice-enough man. I was glad that he was a gentleman.

Finally the train arrived at the depot and I made my way out. Tom had insisted on carrying my luggage and I couldn't believe the hype as we walked through the large station. People were talking in all sorts of language and I was glad I knew enough French to get me by. He hailed a taxi for me to the Le Bristol Hotel and bade me au rvoir.

The Hotel Le Bristol located at 112 rue du Faubourg Saint Honore was in the heart of the art and design fashion district. It was famous for its luxurious interior and its historic architecture. Founded by Rudolf August Oetker, it became one of the most luxurious hotels in Paris in 1877 and it was the place to be for the rich and famous. Coco Chanel, Piet Mondtian, and Pablo Picasso were just a few of the many who frequented its illustrious accommodations.

I was astounded as I entered the doors of this beautiful hotel. My heart was humbled that I was able to witness such beauty. Everywhere I turned was so rich in décor. The ceilings so masterfully done, the walls with gilded framed art, the floor was that of multiple patterns, and statues and live plants were everywhere. The colors mostly of gold, white, and red sent your eyes to another dimension of design. The smells of fresh flowers and a mixture of expensive perfume filled my nostrils.

At that moment in time I gave thanks to my maker for allowing me to experience such beauty. It was another amazing time in my life, the other being the beauty of nature and what it offered. It took my breath away.

I was exhausted from the train ride, ordered room service, and quickly settled down in the most wonderful bed. Even with all the excitement I knew I would have in the morning, I couldn't get the gold out of my head.

I slept till four in the morning and rose to unfamiliar surroundings, but I quickly realized that I was in Paris. The past day's events of travel raced through my mind, and I began to thoroughly wake up. I hadn't made a sightseeing schedule because I wanted to lounge around and do things at my leisure. Just exploring that beautiful hotel probably would take a day and there were many popular shops in the surrounding area to shop in.

I took the elevator down to one of the restaurants and had my choice of everything I could have ever thought could be made for breakfast. The large displays of food stacked high made one's palate salivate and want to try some of everything, even though the origin of some dishes was unknown. With my stomach full, I explored the hotel and oohed and awed at such fine elegance and luxury that I never thought existed.

At about noon, I stepped out to do some shopping at the adjoining shops. Music filled the streets and the smell of food cooking filled the air. Couples were walking hand in hand and some were stopping for a kiss or two. Yes, this was the city of lovers. Memories clouded my mind and I felt so alone and out of place.

They say you never get too old for romance and I was beginning to feel that. I longed for that closeness I had experienced as a young woman. To have that feeling of belonging and needing and being needed by another filled my heart with sadness as I didn't have that. I wondered and questioned myself if I would ever have that again, and if I should have come here to this city of romance.

I shopped till I dropped and went back to the hotel to rest. The dinner menu looked so good that I planned to eat at the hotel. Tomorrow I was going to take the tour bus to the museum and the next day to the Eiffel Tower.

One of the dresses I purchased would be perfect to wear for dinner, so after a soaking bath, I slipped into it. I had to admit that I looked pretty good for a woman of my age. I popped into one of the hair salons and had my hair done up in a popular style. By then I was ravenous hungry and ready to try the gourmet food, no matter what it was made from.

I had my choice of vintage wine and a bottle was brought to my table. I was going to enjoy myself tonight since my bed was right up the stairs. Fancy h'ourderves were served, and I had never tasted anything like them. I was afraid I ate all of them and drank half the bottle of wine. I shouldn't have, because it gave me that warm feeling in my stomach and lightness in my head that was a warning for me to stop.

Dinner came, and what a feast it was—pheasant under glass, tiny onions, green peas, and scalloped potatoes served with a fresh loaf of buttered French bread. Dessert was bread pudding with a wonderful brandy sauce and whipped cream with a cherry atop.

I finished my meal and decided to walk around the hotel before retiring to my room when I noticed someone close to me and I stopped to move in a different direction.

"Mademoiselle, I knew I would find you again." I turned around, and it was the man from the train.

"Bonjour, Tom, so nice to see you again. How did you find me?" I asked.

"I'm staying just down the street and I thought I saw you this morning and I just wanted to see you again," he said.

We strolled around the hotel chatting about all that this wonderful city had to offer. With tired legs, we sat down in one of the sitting areas to rest. Feeling his closeness and the scent of him brought out that feeling I thought I had lost. The warmth of the wine and the atmosphere contributed to that taste of chocolate in my mouth. At that moment we both knew we had to be together to extinguish that fire we both felt. This city was definitely the city for lovers. We made it up to my room. As he closed the door, he gently kissed me and held me as I yielded to his touch. I clung to him, feeling that wonderful sense of sexual excitement creep deeper in my very being. It was so strong that it would have not been possible to stop it. We both were in a time and space where no one or nothing else existed but us and our passion for each other. His kisses were like honey on my lips as he ran his hands up and down my body and then down like electricity seeking the most vulnerable spot. His hot tongue sought the most sensitive area and I was on a trip to the moon. Then he straddled me with his hardness until the trip was completed and we lay back against the pillows with our arms around each other.

Was this all a dream? Was it the wine? Was it Paris? I asked myself. I wasn't going to feel guilty about something that was so wonderful. It made me feel alive again and back from the lonely and dull life I was beginning to find myself in.

Tom and I spent the next three days exploring Paris together and exploring each other sexually like two people on their honey moon. We knew it would have to end soon and each would go back to their everyday lives. I asked no questions of him and he did the same. We were just two lonely people caught up in a romantic city with no cares or thoughts of anyone but ourselves.

—ᵐᵐ—

I arrived back home to London and was glad to be back in my own surroundings. Ted, Brett and Perry had kept a watch on the ranch while I was gone. I felt like going to the cemetery to visit my family that I still missed so much and wondered why they were all gone and I was still here. The Lord must have work for me to do, and I thought I might know just what he intended.

The next day, I went to the soup kitchen to visit and check on everything. My mind was working on how we could expand it to accommodate more people. We needed a bigger pantry as most of the food came in boxed cases, maybe a warehouse just for food. I thought we could build a separate building just to collect and dispense the donated clothing and shoes. Then, too, there needed to be separate quarters for families, single women, and single men.

I had thought about trying to help these people not with just their physical needs, but with their mental needs. I knew it would be a daunting task, but I thought I could just try. I had several retired friends of psychology that may be willing to do some pro-bono work. Of course I was going to donate my time and services, too.

—ᵐᵐ—

I had to see that gold again, so I ventured back into the attic to the empty, locked room and pulled the floor boards up again to the concealed stairway winding down to the large metal safe. I had memorized the combination. As I turned to the last number, it clicked and sprung open, and I was still dazzled at the sight of it. There were tin boxes with gold coins and layers and layers of unstamped gold bars. I looked farther into the alcove and sparkles met my eyes. Jewelry, necklaces, pins, earrings galore shined their brilliance at me with diamonds, rubies, gems, and pearls. This must have been the heirloom jewelry the women wore in the photo albums. I could not believe the Dyland family had amassed such wealth, but how was I going to turn everything into cash? As far as the heirloom jewelry, I am the last of the lineage and there is no one to pass it down to.

It occurred to me that it would not be a good idea to try to cash anything in close to London. I would have to set up another account in an undisclosed city where no one knew me. A bank could refer a financial advisor. Maybe I would take just one or two of the bars at a time. My best bet would be to get an attorney and set up a foundation, the Dyland Foundation.

I turned my attention to Frank and his phobia and thought that maybe I could help him to overcome his fear of being inside for any length of time. In the meantime I was going to have a room built off the ranch house for him since he needed to be close at times. It would be a glass room, so he would not have that closed-in feeling. I didn't know if it would work, but I was going to give it a try.

"Do you know, Frank, why you are afraid of being inside?" I asked.

"No, ma'am," he said, "it's always been this way."

"Do you know how far back you can remember as a child?"

"Maybe around four when my sister told me there was no Santa Clause."

"How old was your sister then?"

"She was five years older than me."

"How well did you take that?"

"I thought she was lying."

"What did you do about it? Did you ask your parents?"

"I only had a mother. My dad had left us. Yes, I did ask her. Yes, she said it was so."

"How did you feel?"

"I wanted to know why everybody was lying. She taught me not to ever lie."

"What did she tell you?"

"It was alright, it was just for kids."

"What kind of a relationship did you have with your mum?

"I loved her, but I hated her."

"Why did you hate her? Did she not take care of you?"

"She had to work a lot, and she left us alone."

"Wasn't your sister old enough to babysit you?"

"Not at first, she was young, too."

"Frank, would you object to being hypnotized by me to help you remember anything catastrophic in your early childhood?"

"No, ma'am, if you think it might help."

We scheduled it for the next two weeks. I felt confident that this was the right path to take to unlock his fear of being closed in. Finding out why was just the beginning. Ending his fear was the kicker.

I made an appointment with a financial advisor, but not in London. I was going back to Paris to get this ball rolling. I knew it was going to take some time to get everything exchanged to either euros or cash and to open an account for the proposed Dyland Foundation. I knew nothing about exchanging gold bars and coins. Some could be sold to collectors, but I wouldn't know how to value it. I knew this had to be handled by trustworthy professionals.

I was hoping I could see Tom again so I could mix business with pleasure. Just the thought of him sent tingles down my spine. He had given me his phone number, and I hadn't called him since I got back. Being busy with the soup kitchen and Frank and figuring out what to do with the gold had taken up the hours. I genuinely liked Tom and wished we lived closer. We could be best friends.

I longed to tell someone about what I found, but I knew that was definitely a no-no.

His phone rang four times, and I was about to hang up when he answered. He was delighted to hear from me, and we set a time and place to meet again. Speaking like southern people I was "in high cotton" and I couldn't wait to see him and to feel his warm embrace and soft kisses.

I enjoyed the train ride just as much as before, maybe more since I was looking forward to seeing Tom again. He didn't know that I had business there and I wasn't going to tell him. I would get things taken care of before we would meet, so my mind would be free to enjoy our time together.

We still knew very little about each other and maybe we should have kept it that way. All I needed to know was that we had an attraction for each other that could not be denied. It was best that way. I would hate to know that he knew that I was the richest woman in the world, because I would feel he was after my money. He might have been married. I didn't want to know. I didn't want to feel any guilt. Maybe he felt the same way.

The first day of arrival was a hectic day, getting all the legal papers drawn up and finding all the information I needed to know to get the bars delivered. I had brought two with me to have them substantiated and to open the account. I really didn't trust any delivery service and made a schedule to bring them myself for deposit in multiple pieces.

I was to meet Tom the next day at the same hotel. He was there, waiting for me with a red rose. He looked as happy to see me as I was to see him. He held me so close that I thought he was going to break me, but I didn't mind. We went into the same restaurant and had a fabulous meal of lamb, roasted broccoli, and carrots served with Chateau Rayas red wine. We talked and talked, and he was such good company. I told him I would be returning from time to time because I had business to take care of here. He honored our agreement to ask no questions and was delighted that he would be able to see me more often. The wine again washed away all my cares of the previous day and I felt so relaxed and glad to be alive to enjoy this wonderful city and to see this handsome man again.

I had asked for the same room as before, where we had found ourselves just or more attracted to each other. The same cologne I hadn't forgotten lingered on his face and neck as we embraced and kissed with long sensual moans. Time was at a standstill, and we were the only people in our world, ready to venture into the universe of passion.

We stayed in my room for the next two days, just calling in room service between our lovemaking, but we both had to return back to our everyday lives. Just knowing this would happen again soon made us not so sad to part.

I returned back home safe and sound and everything seemed to be fine. Frank turned out to be a wonderful groundskeeper. My garden had never been so beautiful and the grounds never looked neater. Again I reveled at this breathtaking estate of my forefathers. They had taken great pains to make it one of the most charmingly elegant mansions ever. I'm amazed that it seems to me that it just fell into my lap. I wished that Mr. Dyland had told my Mum that she was his daughter and that Mary and I were his granddaughters. Little girls need to be able to sit on their grandfather's lap and give and get lots of hugs. It was just memories lost that would have lasted a lifetime for us and for him also. One never knows what goes on in someone else's mind and why they feel so strongly about certain things. Was it the guilt of never claiming my Mum and Aunt as his? Or, was it about honoring his parent's wishes or demands? Maybe he did what my grandmother wanted him to do to—stay away that she was married then. All in all, things came fully out in the end.

I felt like visiting the cemetery, so I picked some fresh flowers out of the garden. Mary always liked daisies and their cheery whiteness with their bright yellow centers. She liked to pick each petal saying, "He loves me, he loves me not" till she got to the last one and being elated if the last one was "He loves me." Mum loved roses and their sweet tantalizing scent and liked to pick the petals and spread them around in the house. The men in my family weren't particular, so I picked some of every kind for them. The cemetery had some real old and tall tombstones dating back to the middle 1700s. The daunting task to research each one was taking a lot of time in seeking answers to the gold.

Some clues to the origin of the gold had to be somewhere in the house, but where? It's such a big house, and I was the only one searching. I had looked through all the journals and photo albums. It's so ironic that so many generations who had lived here didn't know about it, or did they? Maybe there's something behind the portrait of the oldest forefather, the first generation that lived here. I looked at my notes again from the family Bible, read that Joseph Allen Dyland was born in 1769, and compared it to his tombstone. They matched. His portrait was hanging over the fireplace in the library. He was a stern-looking man, about forty-five, with a red beard and mustache and a balding head wearing expensive looking clothes of the era. His cufflinks looked those of gold, and he was wearing a gold bracelet with inlaid rubies. I got a ladder from the kitchen store room, reached to the side of the frame, and pulled it out. Looking for something tacked to the back, I pulled it out farther, but there was nothing there.

I made it a date for the next day to look through the bedrooms. The armoires were still filled with children's christening dresses, crocheted baby caps, booties and sweaters, homemade wooden toys, cribs, and other baby things. This had to be the baby's room, and I was sure nothing would be there.

I ventured on and on to every bedroom and looked again where I thought I might have missed something before to no avail. I just had to let it rest for a while.

—w—

It was time for Frank's therapy session and we settled down to the relaxing outdoor patio. He was nervous, and I worked toward getting myself into my professional mode to try and hypnotize him. My soothing words were the source of getting him to relax and finally going into that state of hypnosis. His expression was of total release of all cares and concern and that drawn look on his face was gone and replaced with a look of peace. As we progressed onward and I asked him questions about his life, that expression turned into almost that of rage, and I had to end the session and bring him back to present consciousness. He awoke feeling great and asked me about what happened, but I thought it best not to tell him.

—⁓—

I was still searching for a clue, any clue, about the gold. I wondered if there were any more hidden rooms in this old humongous house and how many other secrets it might have hidden behind its walls. I looked at all these portraits on the walls and asked them what their life was like and if they had known about the hidden gold. I wondered if they had been spending it gold bar by gold bar just as I intended to do. They would have had to have known because their heirloom jewelry they wore in their photographs was there in the safe with the gold, all except the necklace Mrs. Dyland, my grandfather's mother, wore in her portrait. If my grandfather had known, why didn't he mention it in his will to me? Was it meant to stay in its dark tomb forever, never to be discovered? Did they think it would bring rumors of thievery and disgrace to the Dyland family name?

Tired and famished, I made my way back downstairs to the kitchen, ready to give it up for the day. Mable had left a nice dinner for me, warming on the stove, and I settled down on the sofa to enjoy it with a glass of red wine. Upon finishing the last bite and the last swallow of wine, I fell back on the pillows into a deep sleep.

Dreams of imaginary people of all types and wearing all colors of clothes invaded my sleep. Their clothes were of the fashion worn in the middle seventeen century with men of velvet and silk brocaded frock coats and knee-length britches and with full-sleeve shirts. They wore powdered, curled wigs upon their heads. The women wore hoop dressers with panniers and tight-fitting waist corsets swirling with skirts of lace, ribbons, and flowers and low-cut bodices. Jewelry of sparkling gems bounced up and down on their ears and necks. Their hair was piled high upon their heads, needing support with wire armatures or fake hair. They were dancing in a huge ballroom of giant, white columns and winding stairways and French doors with stained glass windows. Music from an orchestra filled the air with the most beautiful music I had ever heard. Food and wine adorned the white clothed tables with an exquisite array of all types of foods, including a roasted pig complete with the head. I was standing on the stairway, looking down, and a man at the table looked up at me. He was a handsome man of about fifty with a beard and mustache. He was holding a glass of wine and kept staring at me. Feeling uncomfortable, I ran back upstairs into one of the bedrooms and locked the door, thinking he might follow me. The next thing I knew, I was in his arms dancing to that beautiful music. I remembered his face and the English white wig upon his head. I looked down at my dress, and I, too, was dressed like the other ladies. My dress was pink and white satin and was adorned with tiny white roses around the bodice. I could feel the warmth from his body and his breath upon mine, and I seemed to know this man. He had a certain familiarity about him. I no longer felt threatened, but safe in his arms.

I woke up with something on my face. My cat was hungry and he knew how to let me know it. The dream felt so real. I wanted to go back there in that time and with this man who I felt I knew.

As I went about my daily chores, I found myself humming the tune the orchestra was playing in my dreams. I quickly found my tape recorder and recorded it and then planned to go to the music store in town to try to find out any information I could find out about it.

I guess you could say I was an adventurous woman eager to solve mysteries and believed in any signs I thought might be a link or a clue. Maybe this dream was a sign or a lead to just that and I had to follow my dreams, so to speak.

I went through the door of the music store with intent on finding the composer and name of the music I had danced to in my dreams and also when it was recorded for sale. The store clerk ran through his earliest records that being one of Strauss in seventeen hundred fifty. To my dismay, no known music with that tune was to be found. The clerk said that it was so beautiful that I should get an orchestra and record it. I knew very little about music and would have to get someone who read notes better than I to turn it into sheet music. Maybe this could be a challenge later, but I only had one challenge now and it was enough.

The familiarity of the man I danced with in my dreams kept flashing in my mind. That certain way he looked at me and the shape of his eyes puzzled me to no end. *Would I dream of him again?* I asked myself. In the meantime, I picked up my cat and held her close to me. We settled down on the sofa with a good book and a glass of red wine. The constant whirring of the cat's purr and the warmth of the wine slowly put me in a deep slumber.

The light filtering through the windows startled me as I arose abruptly and wondered why I was still on the sofa and not in my bed. As I lay there, I had another idea that day. I quickly showered, dressed, popped a cinnamon roll in my mouth, and sipped a steaming cup of coffee. I was going to look through the sheet music in the music room. I had remembered the words to the music I had heard in my dream: *"Your hair is the color of gold and your eyes are the color of the sea, my bonny girl. I shall find ye and heist ye up, and we shall be rich beyond words, forever and ever, and ye shall wear treasures of diamonds, rubies, and pearls around your neck."* I knew my forefathers were music lovers and apparently with this music room all adorned with different type instruments, they played them themselves. Could one of them have written that music I heard in my dream and which I danced to with that familiar-looking man? It seemed to be just too much. How could something like that come just from a dream?

I could play the piano a little and could read a little of the music. This was something I wanted to get better at. There were stacks of sheet music that I went through. Some were handwritten on brittle paper. Having finished one stack, I moved to the second shelf when one almost fell apart in my hand, but I still could see that it was handwritten. I carefully separated it from the others and set my attention to the written notes and words. I couldn't believe it! They were the same words that I remembered in my dream. "Wait a minute," I asked myself. How could this be happening? I had an eerie feeling. There must be something else happening here, something of a special force guiding me. I took stock of that very minute in time and stood very still and looked all around me. I listened and used all my senses. I didn't feel a cold spot, didn't see anything different, and didn't hear anything either. Quickly I moved to the piano and began to peck the notes out. It took me several attempts, but the melody finally came through so beautifully, just like in my dream. My heart was racing so hard that I thought I might pass out. Just this music, if unpublished, would bring a fortune. I looked for the composer's signature, and there it was—"Joseph Allen Dyland." Of course, his tombstone had a ship carved in it, and I had noticed all through the house that there were replicas of ships.

I pondered over the words of the music "Heist ye up." He wasn't talking about his lover, he was talking about a ship. "Hair of gold and eyes like the sea," meaning expressively the gold on a ship in the sea along with the treasure of diamonds, rubies, and pearls. I thought more and asked myself, "Could Joseph Allen Dyland have been a pirate? If so, which ship did he raid? He would have had to have a crew to help take over the ship and haul out the treasures. Was anybody killed in the process?

My curiosity in the gold and my assumptions finally got me to the point that I didn't want to know anymore. If all of them were true, the name "Dyland" had an ill legacy. If I had my suspicions, most of the family just accepted their wealth without questioning where it originated. Some must have known it, but they kept it a family secret. Otherwise how did the jewels worn by the ladies in the portraits except my grandmother's necklace get in the safe along with the gold and the other jewels? Sometimes it's best to just let things be but maybe anybody else might, but not me.

CHAPTER 17

Frank was not aware of the results of his hypnosis and I thought it best not to tell him. It was obvious, as in many cases, his phobia stemmed from something dramatic in his childhood. We did continue his sessions, and I thought it best not to do hypnosis again right away. The wellness plan was to set a timer and stay indoors ten minutes longer than the time before. It was like a plan smokers use to quit smoking, to wait a little while longer each time between smoking a cigarette. It has worked for some people, and I was hoping it would work for him.

There were many people who frequented the soup kitchen and needed help like Frank. My program to coordinate with therapists who were willing to give their time and expertise was just amazing. The many people who volunteered and coordinated the tasks of scheduling sessions were to be commended greatly. Our team to find paying jobs for the streeters worked tirelessly to get them trained and ready for the working lot. Some weren't mentally ill, but were just down on their luck and needed a helping hand in which we were willing and able to do so.

—⁓—

Still curious about my lineage, I continued to explore the library for anything I could find that not only would give more clues to the origin of the gold but just to anyone who might still be living from the Dyland family. I had not been down in the cellars to do any deep-down exploring, and this old mansion was so big that it would take forever to cover every cranny.

Now that the ranch was not a working ranch anymore, I had plenty of time to lounge around and plan my days of exploration. The next day, I was planning to check one of the cellars out and didn't know just what I would find, probably a whole lot of dust and cobwebs.

The morning brought a drizzling, cold rain as it was nearing wintertime. I got my hot cup of coffee and a piece of buttered toast and sat down at the kitchen table with the morning paper. The only thing in the paper was as almost always, doom and gloom, and it never does anything to get ones day off to a happy start. My cat brushed lazily up against my legs and I reached down and picked her up as she snuggled close to my neck. Animals can be so consoling to one's mood. She certainly loved to love and always boosted my morale.

With my morning ritual of getting dressed warmly, with flashlight in hand and mask covering my face, and my cat following behind me, I ventured into the unknown. The long staircase gave its rickety rackety squeaks and grunts as if saying, go easy on me, I'm very old. I flipped the light switch, and, to my amazement, light shined down through cobwebs that attached themselves to various items stacked on the floor up against the walls, onto other furniture, and odds and ends. I found a broom and began swatting them to make a path through the dusty maze. Even though I had a mask on, dust still penetrated through and I began to cough profusely. I had to get someone down here to clean and organize all the stuff, and there were plenty more items to donate to the church yard sale.

It was like a museum down there. Generations of rich and famous lives sprang out everywhere. Some of the same things that were in the attic were down there, except there were bottles and bottles of wine stored from the seventeen and eighteen hundreds. Fancy feathered hats of men, women, and children were placed on wig forms. Children and baby toys, cribs and old tricycles, quilts, and more trunks were down there, some locked and some not. Old sewing dress forms, one complete with an unfinished dress and spinning wheels with some wool still on it were in just a small space of the enormous basement. If I couldn't find some answers there, I thought, I wasn't ever going to.

I found some empty boxes and began to sort through things for the church sale. Gosh, I could have had enough stuff to open an antique shop, and some would bring a pretty price even at a thrift sale. I picked up each piece by piece and wiped off the dust and cobwebs. That was my thing to do; I loved to plunder through old stuff so I didn't mind the dust. Wondering how long it had been since anyone had been down there, I moved farther with my flashlight and found an old lantern which I lit for more light.

Startled by a mouse that sprang out from under an old piece of furniture, I made my way to one of the locked trunks. I had brought a crowbar with me, pried the rusty lock off, and swung the top up and back. Dust flew everywhere, and I had to step back a few minutes to let it settle. There were old books, papers, and clothes of all sizes for men, women, and children. I found nothing of any significance here, so I moved on to another one.

The second trunk was larger and more sturdily built, and, of course, the lock was thicker and harder to break. After my third try, it finally popped loose. It contained equipment used to navigate a ship, and my suspicions were beginning to bear out. Discovering all that added fuel to the fire in me to keep on with my search for answers. I dug deeper and deeper into the trunk and saw something wrapped in an old piece of cloth. It was some kind of a gun of olden times. There was an old tattered leather book lying next to a sword with a ruby-studded ivory handle. I opened it carefully. It seemed to be a ship captain's log book. The name was Captain Joseph Allen Dyland of the ship "Destany," Ringsend, Dublin City, Ireland, June 16, 1793. There were the usual written daily records of passenger names and position, course of speed, weather, and events. I kept flipping till I got to the last page of June 30, 1793. "We are approaching a stalled pirate ship hung up on a reef, flying a yellow flag, The Wayjourner." No other information was recorded on that date.

I was very excited as I ran up the stairs to the library to search the many books on ships. Finally I found the right one that had a list of ships that had sailed the Celtic Sea. Sure enough; there was one listed as a pirate ship that had gone down and never recovered on June 30, 1793, "The Wayjourner." My suspicions were no longer suspicions. It was said to have contained the confiscated treasures of fifty ships.

My curiosity had always been a trait I thought was a good thing in that I learned a lot of things by acting on it. That was not the case this time. I was sure that many lives were lost, if not by being shot or stabbed, then by being drowned. I could only pray for my forefather that God will somehow forgive him. I was wondering if he had ever thought about how he acquired this great fortune and was he ever able to enjoy it. One good thing was coming out of it: It was now being used for the good of mankind. God rest his soul.

—m—

I had given Frank a log to keep his extra time he spent inside each day. A month had passed since he had been hypnotized and I felt like it was enough time to check his progress or nonprogress. He came in the door smiling, and I knew that he was ready to give me a good report, and a good report it was. He had been able to spend an extra half hour each day under a roof and I was so proud of him. I set the time up another extra fifteen minutes, and he seemed to think he could make it without too much frustration. As time went by, I gave him the challenge of extending the time more each month till he was able to function normally inside. Giving him something to do in the allotted time helped him tremendously. The mind works in mysterious ways.

As I continued to go about my days, I caught myself humming the tune of the hand written music I found in the music room. I vowed that I would learn to play it better since it was such a magnificent melody. There was no title to it, and I was going to think up one for it. I knew it had to be a special one. It was still a mystery to me that Joseph Allen composed this beautiful music and never recorded it that I knew of and I could never find any record on the charts that he did.

I really didn't know how to go about having it recorded, especially since I didn't write it, so I went to see an attorney. He advised me to get a patent on it to be safe. A song can be copyrighted up to seventy years from the end of the calendar year in which the composer or author of the music died. I certainly had that amount of time and more covered. I was to have a copy of the handwritten notes or an audio recording placed in an envelope that was signed with my name across the seal of the envelope. I was to mail it to myself by registered mail. The stamped posted date would serve as a vital point in the event of a disputed copyright. It was very important that I do not open the envelope but store it in a safe place if I should ever need it in any legal proceedings.

The challenge of naming the song weighed heavily on my mind, and getting an orchestra to play it was getting to be an obsession for me. I couldn't believe how beautiful it was and I couldn't wait to hear an orchestra play it with its many instruments. The question of having someone sing it or just leaving it as an instrumental was a task in itself

Over the next several weeks, I thought and thought about the name I should give the song. It had the smooth and gentle vibes of a love song, soft and slow, flowing like love should be. It put one in the mood for the nearness of a lover's arms around you and a warm gentle kiss upon your neck. Was my forefather, the composer, in love with someone when he wrote it? I always figured that anyone who had written a beautiful love song had to have been in love themselves to have written such a passionate melody.

Sometimes I think that I was born too late. I would have loved to have been born in that time and space and to have known him, but maybe not his secrets.

Knowing that I had to have a title for the song before I had an orchestra to record it, I spent the rest of the day and night pondering many possible ones. I went through a complete notebook scratching out this and that one and finally settling on a possibly five. I settled on one: "MY BONNY GIRL"

The words to the song were:

Your hair is the color of gold,
Your eyes the color of the sea,
My bonny girl, my bonny girl,
I shall find you, and we shall be rich beyond words.
My bonny girl, my bonny girl,
And ye shall wear jewels of diamonds and pearls.
My bonny girl, my bonny girl,
Love is like a warming sun,
Waiting to capture ones lonely heart,
It is I who wait with open arms,
For my bonny girl, my bonny girl.
For my bonny girl, my bonny girl.

Everyone loved the song and was eager to play it. With all the instruments, it sounded so enchanting that my heart just melted and that old nostalgic feeling of my lost loves came back to haunt me. I missed that young love feeling of two people hopelessly in love that you felt like you would die if you were apart. Sometimes life does not seem fair to have that ripped from you not once but twice.

All the legal aspects of the recording were now taken care of, and it was ready for production. I was on pins and needles waiting to hear it for the first time on the radio, and hear it I did. It was in so much demand that it couldn't be produced fast enough to get in the stores. I was truly blessed again, and truly thankful.

CHAPTER 18

I found myself wanting to see Tom again and I needed to take some more gold bars to the Paris bank. We had agreed not to get too involved with each other, but I wanted to share the news about the music. I would never divulge the secret of the house to anyone.

The train came rolling to a stop and I watched the many passengers descend down the steps, ready to meet their loved ones or step on into the London station. It was scheduled to depart again for Paris in fifteen minutes, and I was looking forward to getting away and see the countryside again as well as Tom. It was always good to have someone to talk to and to have dinner with and to share our friendship. He was a delightful, kind, and considerate man, and I was trying not to fall in love with him, yet I knew nothing about his life nor he mine.

The train ride was pleasant as always with all the beauty of nature, and the weather was beginning to turn to spring. I felt the soft cool breeze on my face as I stepped from the platform and smelled the fresh Paris air. Tom was waiting for me, wearing a stylish French suit and a derby hat with a small red feather tucked under the band. I didn't realize that I would be so thrilled to see him again as I ran to his arms. The tightness of his warm embrace told me that he was really glad to see me again, too. He hailed a cab and we went straight to the hotel restaurant for lunch.

It felt good to be back in Paris. I loved London and my ranch, but there was something magical about Paris, perhaps it had a lot to do with Tom. Having someone to see all the sights with and have dinner with made it perfect.

We settled down at a corner table with fresh daffodils and tulips. All the sounds and smells of food, people, and dishes clanging made up this thing called "life." There was a familiar tune being played by a small trio, and I recognized it right away. It was "My Bonny Girl."

Tom commented on it right away, "What is that beautiful music?"

I answered, "It's called 'My Bonny Girl' and it was written by one of my great grandfathers. I found it among some sheet music, handwritten and signed by him. It's a long story as how I came about finding it."

"I've got plenty of time. Why don't you tell me about it?" he said. I told him about the dream, but not all of it. I still could not trust anyone to tell about the gold.

We were talking about motion pictures and he asked me about the one that was filmed in London a few years ago. I debated on telling him that it was about my family. I didn't want him to know that much about my life and where I came from. I knew if I did, he would know that I was a very rich woman. I wanted him to love me for me and nothing else. Our agreement was to ask no questions and just enjoy each other's company.

We finished our delicious meal and walked the streets of Paris, looking in this shop and that shop. Tom wanted to purchase a record of "Bonny Girl." The park was close by, so we walked there, sat on a park bench, and talked for a long time. We so enjoyed each other's company and it was such a nice deliverance from my everyday routine.

We arrived back at the hotel in our same room and ordered tea and small cakes from room service. Afterward, we took a long, soaking bath with each other in the massive tub. His arms wrapped the fluffy towel around me as we fell upon the bed. The hot bath was only a perquisite of what followed. Our hot bodies entwined around each other and our passion ignited with the urgency of too-long-denied desires.

We said our farewells the next morning and I made my way to the Paris bank. I was glad I could make these deposits to the Dyland Foundation. Its strength was growing each day and was earning a good interest. Soon we would be able to start new soup kitchens in different communities. I was even thinking about our furry friends—dogs and cats; they needed help, too.

Royalties were beginning to come in from "My Bonny Girl" and so as to say it "sweetened the pot." I was still receiving royalties from our family movie, too. I looked all around me at this beautiful and wonderful world and thanked God for what was given. How could one person be so blessed as to have so much that I could help so many?

I was glad to be back home to check on Frank and the ranch. Believe it or not, I found him inside cooking dinner. What a good sign that was, and he seemed genuinely comfortable and not rushing to get back outside. We shared his not-bad dinner and discussed everything that happened while I was gone and what needed to be done in the coming week. Spring was beginning to blossom, flower beds needed working, and a general clean up after the cold winter months was required.

—⚹—

While checking through my mail, I found a personal post postmarked from Ireland. I thought it strange, since I knew no one from there. It was from a Ms. Ross from Dublin. It read:

Dear Ms. Blankley,

You don't know me, but I saw the movie "Desperation" of your family, and in it was the part about the Dyland family. Mind you, I am not a fortune seeker and hope not

to be thought of as one by writing this letter. I only want
to meet with you and discuss my reasons for contacting
you. Please, if you are interested, my address is: Marilyn
Ross 1638 Forsythe Street, Dublin, Ireland.

I had no idea what she would like to talk to me about, but my curiosity again got the best of me and I went to my secretary and wrote a post to her. Our appointment to meet in my library was set for the following week. The next several days, my head was full of reasons she might need to see me, but none of them seemed to be very important. I tried to recall anyone whom I knew by that name, but none came to mind. I hoped that she wasn't a publicity or fortune seeker, because that would not sit well with me at all. Could she be a long lost heir to the house ready to take the mansion from me? Just to be safe, I wanted Frank to be close around the day of her arrival.

The day finally arrived and I had butterflies in my stomach. About 3 p.m. I heard the bell ring from the front gate and I disengaged the lock for her to drive up to the main house. She was an attractive woman, about fiftyish, slim, and very stylish with a tan suit and medium high heels. She was carrying a black briefcase. Her hair was curled up in a bun upon her head. She wore a gold cross necklace and a gold wedding band, but no other jewelry. I could smell her flowery perfume as she descended toward me.

"I'm Marilyn Ross, but please call me Marilyn," she said.

"I'm Anna Blankley, but you can call me Anna."

I offered her refreshments as she had driven for seven hours from Dublin. We exchanged all the niceties that polite women exchange upon just meeting each other, and she came across to me as being professional but very personable. Frank brought tea, sandwiches, and cakes, and we settled down in the comfy chairs in the large library. After more compliments about the house and surroundings, she began to get down to the reason for the visit.

"Perhaps you have heard of the Organization for Adopted and Misplaced Children?" she asked.

"Yes," I replied, "but not much."

"It's an organization funded by the government and originated after the onslaught of First World War when so many children were displaced either from the loss of their parents from dying from diseases and getting killed on the battlefield or bombings. Well, I have been working for it for the last twenty-five years, and I have come upon some records of your family on your mother's side. I got interested in them when I saw your movie and working with adoption and lost children it raised some questions that most people would never even think of. In my line of work, some things aren't always as they seem."

I sat and watched her. Seeing her so serious and intent on telling me some very important information, my mind was swirling out of control. I knew it had to be something about my Mum. I thought all the mystery of who my real mum was had been solved, but what about my aunt who had impersonated her? Then it could be about Mr. Dyland, maybe he wasn't my real grandfather after all, and he had willed all this by deception. I held my breath as she opened her briefcase and brought out a handful of papers.

"Correct me if I'm not right as I go over all this information with you," she said. "It is to my understanding that Maggie Smith was an orphan back in 1900 in London, England, and Olivia Blankley was her alleged twin and their mother was Rebecca Jonestone. Maggie Smith impersonated Olivia who died from a fall and took over the role of mother to you, Anna Blankley, and to your sister, Mary Blankley, and the role of wife to your father, Colin Blankley. Am I right so far?"

I nodded my head with tears in my eyes and answered a soft "yes." What could this woman be telling me that I didn't already know? Why had she come here in my home to ask me all these questions that I have tried my best to put behind me? As she looked at me, I could tell she hated to dredge up all this past history that was so harrowing for me to face again. The look in her eyes told me that she was a gentle woman with a job that was sometimes against her gentle and tender nature.

"I have a copy of the police report of the finding of your mother's body. I hate to put you through all this, and I hope you don't feel ill of me for coming here. When you hear what I've discovered, I think you will feel different, and this information will somewhat answer questions you didn't know were there."

She lowered her eyes back to the paper she held in her hand.

"Most adoptive parents require that the records be sealed for an indefinite period of time or until the adopted child reaches the age of adulthood. I dug and found some interesting information among some records from some of the ravaged bomb-struck buildings. It was the will of your grandmother, Rebecca, that your mother's twin, Maggie Dyland, be adopted by John and Caroline McKnight in 1900. By gathering of this information substantiated by these records, it is my assumption that Maggie Smith was not your Aunt. Maggie Smith seemed to be so desperate for a family that she truly believed she was your mother's twin. Apparently she did look amazingly like her, so amazingly that she pulled it off very well, and I think she believed she was. Maybe it could have been because both you and Mary were very young and your father had been away for four years and people change in that amount of time. I am here to tell you that I did some more research on your real aunt, Maggie, and sad to tell you that she passed away in 1919. I don't know what you can do with this information, if anything, but at least you know the true facts and you can now begin to put all the pieces of your family together. If there are any questions about what I've told you, please feel free to check them out yourself or have an attorney. There is now being developed a test for DNA to determine the lineage of a person and you only need one of the person's hair and you might want to look into it."

She began to sip her tea as I tried to let all she had told me sink in. What a lot to learn about Maggie Smith and to learn that my grandmother did not put my Aunt Maggie in an orphan home at all. I only hope that she was adopted by a loving couple and that she had a good rearing. It was all sad that the twins did not ever know each other and even sadder that my Mum died so young. Could I still have such resentment toward Maggie Smith knowing what I just learned and that it could turn into hate? Is there such a fine line between the love for someone that played the role of your loving mother or the hate you feel for her after discovering that she misled everyone. There was still one last question that had been lingering in my mind: Did she kill my mum? Did she get away with murder? This was a question I will never know the answer to.

I knew Marilyn had had a long day, and I asked her to stay the night. Frank had made some of his vegetable soup, and she was delighted to stay. I felt like having someone to talk to that night and she was a warm, sensitive person to keep company with. I also missed that relationship of one woman to another for company. I also knew I probably would have more questions she could help me with.

Thinking of poor Dad and about how he would have felt knowing that his wife, Olivia, our mother, was not her, but an imposter, made my heart soar with pain. If he had only known and if Mary and I had only known she was lying in that old dug well behind the barn. I cringed and just couldn't have imagined it. What a horrible thing to happen to our Mum. I wondered how many more secrets my life held and how many would I find the answers to.

Marilyn said her goodbyes the next morning and thanked us for the hospitality. I watched her as she drove down the driveway. The information she brought with her changed my life again and stirred up more sadness than I thought I wouldn't be able to handle. I went back into the house to my bedroom and had a good cry till I thought I had no more tears left. I kept hearing Marilyn's words, "I don't know what you want to do with it. There is a DNA test now available." I rushed to Maggie's old room. It was just the same as she had left it. I could still smell the talcum powder she used after her bath. There was her robe still hanging over the rocking chair she often sat in. Her box of chocolates she loved to snack on was beside her bed. The bouquet of fresh flowers we picked for her each day was all brown, wilted, and falling down upon her dresser. We had loved this woman and she had guided us through all our growing-up days, soothing us when we had little girl problems, and advising us when we became teenagers and later into adulthood. She was a loving wife to our father and always cuddling around his neck and making sure he felt loved. She would make his favorite desserts and was always ready to please him with even the smallest things. I asked myself, how could I judge this woman, but there was that curiosity that I thought was a curse sometimes, and it was bearing heavy on my mind.

I made my way to Maggie's dresser and opened the top drawer where she had kept her hair brush and pulled a handful of hair from it. I found a handkerchief and wrapped it carefully, folded it, and placed it in an envelope. I was then ready to find out more about that DNA testing. Looking around Maggie's room before I left and closed the door brought back all those memories that were now tainted with regret and sadness of things that could have been different.

I went to see my attorney, Jack Baker, who was also an old friend, to discuss what I had learned from the last few days. He was shocked and agreed that I should go ahead with the DNA testing. He had heard good reports of the test being accurate, and it could determine the paternal and maternal genetic blueprint. It was developed by the British scientist, Alec Jeffreys, and, as a result, had solved a lot of crimes. I was willing to give it a shot, and Jack made all the necessary measures to get the sample to the proper venues.

It had been several weeks and I still hadn't heard anything from the testing lab. My nerves were on edge more and more each day that the results did not arrive. The next day I received a letter stating that I should receive the results the following week. At least now I knew they were working on it and it wasn't stuck back on a shelf somewhere. I would be able to relax and not rush to the post until next week.

—⁓—

The weather was beginning to cool and Frank was raking leaves and cleaning dead foliage from the many flowers and shrubs. I felt like those spent flowers that had now lost their vibrancy and fell like the leaves on the ground to their death. I found solace in the woods surrounding the ranch and to the creek and springs that flowed into the lake as I walked many miles. I would watch the squirrels rushing around with acorns and hickory nuts in their mouths readying for wintertime. The ducks on the ponds would sail in the evenings to their safe nesting place on the island. In the mornings, I would see them leaving out just as graceful, flying as they had come in in the evenings. Being there surrounded by God's nature was the most soothing feeling I could ever have had. With the wind and sun on my face, I forgot all my troubles and all the iniquities imposed by Maggie. I vowed at that moment no matter what the DNA test proved, to forgive her and live the rest of my life being thankful for the love I gave my family and for the love they most generously gave to me.

The DNA test came on a Friday of the following week. The Organization's caseworker would have never approached me with Maggie's case unless she was certain. I held it in my hand not wanting to really know the results but curious as always. As I carefully opened it, I could barely see through my tears and I was almost certain of the results. My fears barred out with my reading: "NOT A BIOLOGICAL MATCH."

How could all of us, me, Mary, and Dad, and everyone else not realize that she was not Mum? True, we were young and Dad just thought that she had changed since he hadn't seen her in four years. I believe she truly believed that she was my Mum's twin and she took the opportunity to be part of a family that she had never had.

I bowed my head and prayed for God to give me the strength to forgive Maggie and to keep my mind from thinking that she might have committed murder. I thanked him again for my many blessings and to let the rest of my life be filled with the spirit of giving to others. I prayed for my forefathers if their fortune was gotten by piracy and murder. I prayed for this country and for the cure for the many diseases that have swept and ravaged the world and for all the political unrest. I prayed for Maggie and my poor Mum. God rest their souls. It's a new day, a new gift, and I intended to untie the ribbons.

The new day was sunny and bright with just a slight cool to the breeze. I looked upon the world now a little different after discovering the last secret of Maggie. I wondered if there would be any more and if there were, I hoped they would be good ones. *But what was I going to do with this information?* I asked myself. Since all the family was gone, it didn't matter whether I had even found out about this latest secret. I guess it was good for me to know, but it just brought up more mixed feelings.

My kitty was brushing against my legs. I picked her up and snuggled her close to my neck. Her love was undeniable and un-ending, and I could always rely on her for a warm hug and a soft meow. I ran my fingers over her soft, long hair and thanked God for this small form of life that I felt he had created just for me. It's as if he knew people like me needed these small bundles of fur to keep the calm in their souls and the warmth in their hearts.

CHAPTER 19

Paris was calling me again and I made plans to leave the next morning. I had already called Tom to meet me at the train station. I wanted so to tell him about my life and everything about me, and I wanted to learn everything about him. I knew we had agreed to keep our relationship just that and just enjoy each other's company. If he was married, I did not want to know, and by not knowing, I didn't have to feel any guilt. I just knew that he was a warm, sensitive man and was becoming a wonderful friend, but we both knew the distance between us would be a factor and neither of us wanted to leave our homes.

Tom was leaning against a lamp post as I stepped down from the train. He was his same handsome self and I was beginning to realize how important he was becoming to me. He looked at me with that same winning smile on his face and I sent mine right back to him and I thought at that moment just how wonderful life could be. I still had many more ribbons to untie.

We walked to the hotel and went to the same restaurant for lunch. Oh, how I loved Paris and all the glamour of the city. It made me feel young again, and I reveled in everything it had to offer. After a delicious lunch, as always, we strolled hand in hand on the snow covered streets to the park. The fresh, cold air was refreshing as it kissed my cheeks and I breathed it in like fine perfume. It was like a winter wonderland of sparkling diamonds with the sun shining its golden rays upon the layers of whiteness. With Tom's warm hand in mine, I felt like a school girl on her first date. It's true a gentle human touch has a power beyond anything else imaginable. It can make one feel loved, cared for, concerned about, and many other calming feelings necessary for the control of our hearts and souls. Tiny birds were scurrying around, trying to find a tidbit or two of crumbs left by people strolling by and little green sprouts of daffodils were beginning to poke their heads above the snow in anticipation of spring flowering. We stopped to admire a large tree and the vastness of it with its towering limbs jacketed with snow and looking like an overgrown and misshaped one from a fairytale. This winter wonderland transformed us into a different world as we stopped and looked into each other's eyes. Being here was just like heaven and we both felt the magic of being in love as we kissed, held each other, and felt the pounding from our hearts.

Our lovemaking that night was gentle, and we responded to each other like we had time unending to make the joy of our union last, for we were indeed in a time and dimension all of our own. No one else existed for us and the closeness of our bodies was all that mattered as we breathed in each other's breath.

Later that night, we talked about our lives and I told Tom about what I had found out about my Aunt. He had not seen the movie or had not put it together that it was about my Mum, and I preferred to keep it that way. He did not know that it was she who had impersonated my Mum. I just told him that she had impersonated my Aunt. He was appalled that she would do such a thing and that she got away with it for such a long time, and he would make it a point to see it.

We said our farewells the next morning and I rambled on to the bank with my gold bars. I wanted to check on the balance of the account and get some information on a reputable auction house. There was still the large chest of jewels that I needed to liquefy. Some of the necklaces and rings, I knew, must have belonged to royalty. The diamonds and gems were exquisite, and I was tempted to keep them for myself, but I could never enjoy wearing them after knowing how they were gotten. I knew that I must have them appraised piece by piece before auctioning, just a few sets at a time.

I left that afternoon on my journey back home and my thoughts were about Tom and each moment we were together. He put such joy in my life. I thanked God for him and his sweetness, gentleness, and love. I wished we lived closer together, but I could not ever see leaving my beautiful Rosehaven. Paris is a vibrant city and I enjoyed visiting, but I needed the serenity of the farm and its quiet solitude.

—ɷ—

That night, I settled close to the hot fire of the fireplace in my soft sofa with a hot cup of tea, and, as usual, my kitty in my lap. All sorts of thoughts were floating through my mind. The thoughts were of my real Mum, Olivia, and what would she have been like as my Mum? I had bits and pieces of her from my early childhood, but I have often wondered if she would have been anything like Maggie. I have several pictures of her when she was a teenager and the resemblance to Maggie was amazing. I can't blame Maggie for thinking that they may have been twins and she was never questioned or no one noticed the difference. People didn't travel much in those days for fear of catching diseases, and they mostly stayed at home. Transportation was not like it was today, and many women never learned to drive.

The jewels were first and foremost on my mind and quite a challenge as to how I was going to turn them into euros. I knew this had to be handled very carefully indeed. If these were jewels belonging to the Queen, there might still be some reward for them or any information leading up to their disappearance. It could be that even after all these years, there could be maybe some information just waiting on them to surface. I could be in deep trouble for having stolen jewels in my possession. I could be arrested and jailed. *Surly not*, I told myself, after all these many years, but I didn't want to take the chance. I thought maybe I should just leave them locked up in their dark and gloomy tomb and just forget about them. Thinking about how I could use the cash to help the underprivileged made me think of another plan.

I still thought that a lot of answers were in the journals and photo books or somewhere in this house. I focused on the jewelry worn by the ladies of the house in the portraits and photo albums. They were the same jewelry that was in the safe except the one my grandmother wore. The large portraits hanging together on the entrance wall of all the ladies of the house wore the same necklace; the one that held the secret code to the safe. That told me that everyone who lived in the house knew about the safe and its treasure. Some of the shelves of the stacked bars had bare spaces and there were a few bare shelves. I figured at one time all the shelves were probably filled to capacity. Still I wondered if my grandfather knew about it. And if he did, why didn't he let me know somehow. He was in everyone's eyes a fine and reputable person. Maybe he didn't want us to discover any sins of our ancestors that would tarnish the Dyland name and make us feel ashamed of the wealth we inherited. If he only knew I wouldn't blame him for anything and I wouldn't feel any less admiration for him. I just wish I had known that he was my grandfather, so I could love him like a granddaughter loves her grandfather.

I went to the attic to the safe to look at the jewels again, thinking I would start with three sets. Being stored so long, they needed cleaning, and I wondered if any more of them might have a secret compartment. I planned on taking them to my jeweler the next day and hoping he would abide by his code of ethics. I could trust him. I thought I should probably look into having a gemologist appraise them and maybe having more than one appraisal from a different one.

I rambled around deep in the treasure chest and found a cloth bag thin with age and as I looked into it, I found it was full of diamonds. I gasped at the sight of them as I poured some out in my hand. The brilliance of them shined from the light I held in my hand. They took my breath away. Looking at all that wealth made my head light. I had to sit down and I knew in my heart that this had to be stolen from a pirate ship. My great-great-great grandfather, Joseph Allen Dyland was not only a pirate but also a pirate who stole from fellow pirates' ship. I had no answer as how to begin to return all this to its rightful owners, because they were all dead. The gold bars had no markings on them. I had no idea who it would have belonged to anyway. I think maybe he sunk the ship after raiding it, and it was never found. *So what should I do?* I asked myself, *Carry on with my plan and use multiple banks?*

I made an appointment with my jeweler the next day to have the three sets cleaned and appraised by him, hoping he wouldn't ask any questions. But I cancelled my appointment and arranged for a gemologist to come to my home and appraise them on site. I had heard that there had been occasions where some jewelers would change out the genuine stones and replace them with loo-kalike fake ones; I just didn't want to take that chance.

While all this was exciting, it was unnerving and exhausting for me. I felt like I needed to take a few days break and I went to the soup kitchen to see how things were going. I had a plan to go down in the cellar on the west end of the house when I returned. Oh how I wished Mary was still here to do all this exploring with me. She would have been in plundering heaven. Not being able to share all this with anyone was taking a toll on me. She was a wonderful sister, and we had shared everything with each other throughout all our lives. I missed all my family. Being alone and living in this great big mansion was very lonely, and I thought of them daily. Sometimes I thought I got a glimpse of one of them from around a corner or heard someone's voice. Their presence was still here like all the memories and I found peace in them. Their love surrounded me and wrapped their warm spirits in my very being. I knew I would join them in their glorious heaven one day and we would be a happy family once again.

—∽—

I rested for the next several days trying to clear my mind and exercise my body. Walking in the woods and breathing the fresh air always soothed me and made me feel better. After walking for a few miles, I sat down on a tree stump, hoping to see some wildlife. The sun felt good on my face as it was the middle of spring. The air danced around me, taunting me with its sweet fragrance, and I breathed it in like a fine perfume that only could be produced from the forest and the fields of wildflowers. As I lay very still, a family of white-tail deer came out of the shadows of the trees and pranced nonchalantly toward the creek. Their gracefulness always amazed me and their constant awareness of their surroundings reminded me of characters out of a fairytale. I picked some wildflowers and made my way to the cemetery to visit my family.

I slept fitfully the next night and arose early to start my next adventure into the unknown. After a hot cup of tea and crackers, I fed my cat, and we ventured down the stairs into the next cellar. This cellar had a few steps that needed to be repaired, but I was careful, and made a mental note to have them replaced. My light illuminated more cobwebs and similar items as in the attic and the other cellar. I did find a light switch and I switched it on to see farther in the corners. There were more old trunks down here and most of them were ship trunks with large metal locks on them. As before, I had learned to bring a crowbar to open stuff with, because I would never find matching keys and my fast curiosity would not allow me to spend hours looking for them. I found lots of items relating to ships, periscopes, navigation equipment. One had a metal disc that had a scale with degrees and a ruler for measuring the latitude and by the noon altitude of the sun and the declination of stars. There was a sextant which measured the angle of a star, planet, sun, or moon in the Verizon, and it was useful for allowing users to determine their latitude within a mile or two in the sea. Sea captains had to be very skilled to use all these equipment as if not they could be led off course for miles.

I found more sea-related items, a captain's cap and uniforms, gloves, rain gear, boots, lots of ropes. The next trunk had some of the similar items, but lots of souvenirs purchased from different ports. There were books about different seaports and maps. I found a metal can full of photographs that I tried not to look at. Apparently grandpa had a thing for native women and their young brown bodies stared back at me as I blushed. As I dug deeper, I found what I was looking for—a journal of Joseph Allen Dyland. My heart was pounding. I had to sit back a few minutes to catch my breath. As I stared at the tattered and worn leather-bound journal, I felt like I had found my way from being lost on a long and winding road that I had traveled which I had no idea where I was or had been. I hopefully held in my hand the answers which I had searched for and I prayed to God that my suspicions of murderous foul play by my great grandfather were totally unfounded.

Looking no farther in the trunk, I closed the lid as I rose and took the book upstairs. Carefully placing it on the table by the sofa, I ate a simple dinner and set my sights on a night filled with the long-awaited knowledge I hoped to learn. It read:

THE JOURNAL OF JOSEPH ALLEN DYLAND

Born July 17, 1769

The date of today is July 7, 1795.
I thought today would be a good date to start my life's journal. So far my life has been good and I have had good parents who have given me a good education in banking. Lately, I have become restless and hankering to get out from inside buildings and enjoy the nature of

God. I have always been fascinated with ships and the sea and always wanted to sail my own ship on the high seas. I am giving notice of a departure of work tomorrow and I intend to purchase my own ship.

July 20, 1795
I don't intend to keep a daily account of my life, but of the most important events affecting my life and today is most important, because I have purchased that ship and named it "Destany." I'm so excited and have hired an ex-seaman to teach me everything I need to know about captaining a ship.

October 29, 1795
My first voyage is today on the Celtic Sea along with my crew of ten. Weather is good and we hope to have some fair sailing and good fishing.

November 5, 1795
Everything is good and I am enjoying the sailing; crew is in good spirits; returning home in one week.

November 7, 1795
Plans have changed. We discovered a ship flying a black flag which meant they were pirates and if you surrender, there will be minimum loss of life. They were also flying a red flag which meant if you try to resist, no life will be spared. Another flag, a yellow flag was flying, which meant it was a death ship. This meant that everyone was stricken with some deadly disease. We saw no sign of life and the ship has run on a reef. We have watched it, and no crew was visible. The crew and I know from its size that it contains valuables pirated from other ships and we discussed the possibility of boarding it, but

there is a possibility of contracting the plague ourselves. One crewmember, John, volunteered to go aboard and search for their treasures for ten percent more of the take. He had to be protected from the deadly disease, so we devised a plan and we doused him with rum and covered his mouth up with a doubled bandana. We all waited for what seemed like hours, thinking that maybe someone was still alive and had captured or killed him. Finally we watched him as he climbed back aboard our ship dancing with thumbs up and holding up something. He found it hard to get the word "GOLD" out. All the crew whooped, hollered, and danced around, but after all the excitement, they came to the realization that it was on a death ship. We made our volunteer strip off his clothes and we burned them and threw him in the drink to wash off, when he came back aboard, we scrubbed him and threw him back to rinse off. We had a lot to talk about and to ask John what he saw. He said the stench was horrible and he guessed the ship had been marooned at least three days by the condition of the three bodies he saw. And, of course, the rest of the crew would have been already disposed of by burial at sea. The next question was: Would my crew consider boarding the ship to get the treasure? We had to think on this a lot and how would we get it without contracting the disease ourselves and dying, too.

November 8, 1795
The weather was cold and it began to snow, but everyone had one thing on their minds, "gold" and if it would be worth the risk of dying. John told us that it was a huge haul, probably stolen from another pirate ship or ships. That's what they did, they stole from each other and

the size of the ship indicated that they could dominate the waters.

We had a tough decision to make, either be rich or dead, and we chose to be rich. It took us two days to figure out how we could do it. If we left and came back, we took the chance of another ship discovering it and maybe them taking the chance and getting the treasure. It all came back to the rum, it would kill anything. Having at least a couple barrels of rum was a must for any captain to have on his ship; otherwise he would not have a crew. We knew there was a time factor, and we did not want to be discovered. Giving up their rum was worth being rich, and the plan was set in place for tomorrow. We would soak our clothes in the germ-killing nectar, soak our heads, rub it into our skin, soak our doubled bandanas for our masks, soak our gloves, and spray our boots with it.

November 9, 1795
We put our plan in place and prayed that it would work. I think we all got tipsy, but we were serious and cautious, and the very thought of getting rich beyond words kept us at our height of attention.

I went first to assess the situation and see exactly what the treasure consisted of and how much. John had spent so long a time first checking the ship out, because he had to figure how to get the giant safe open. At last he had gone through the pockets of the long dead captain to get the key and had to wait till his nausea had subsided before he could open it. I almost fell to my knees as to what I saw. There were stacks and stacks of gold bars and gold bullion, coins, trunks full of jewels, bolts and bolts of silk, satin and lace, Persian rugs, silver cups and tea sets, pottery, paintings from famous artists, and all sorts of other valuables.

I went back to my ship and reported what I had seen. The crew roared with joy and was raring to fetch it and get away before another ship showed up. We had to get all the vessels we could find to put it all in.

It took us all the rest of the day to remove all we could get. We left the bolts of materials and anything else that we thought may harbor the sickness germs and set the ship on fire with their drums of rum. As soon as we got back on board, we soaked everything we got with rum. We immediately changed our rum laden clothes and threw them in a pile and burned them and jumped in the freezing water to wash off.

Worrying that the smoke from the burning ship would attract other ships on the scene, we left for a small cove I knew that was hidden from the main route. How lucky could we get, we thought? Now if we just don't get sick and we knew that time would tell.

November 10, 1795
Everyone seemed to feel no ill effects from the day before except some had some slight skin burn from the rum. We were more than ready to count our treasure. We divided the bars between us. Since it is my ship, I got ten percent more as well as John for volunteering to go aboard first. We had no quarrels among us as there was more than enough for all of us to be rich for generations.

November 20, 1795
We all stayed at the sea for the quarantined time in order not to spread anything to our families. Luckily no one contracted the disease and all we did was party since we still had a full barrel of rum. Everyone was

in a dream world, planning on how they were going to spend their fortune. We figured out that we might need to move to another city or country, in order not to raise suspicions, and spend wisely at first. I would have gladly returned everything if only I knew who to return it to.

November 22, 1795
We sailed back toward home without seeing another ship. Everyone was still well and very thankful that we all dodged the sickness. I stressed to everyone about being discreet, and they all agreed with me.
The middle of the night was the best time for us to anchor back as quickly as possible to unload the goods. We had decided to get a horse and wagon and load it all up under cover. We then would take it to John's big barn and hide it till we could divide it all and each take their part.

November 23, 1795
When we arrived at John's barn, we were all very cold and exhausted and immediately fell asleep in the hay.

November 24, 1795
Today was the day each one of us got our share. We officially declared ourselves beyond rich. We had to make more plans as to how we were going to get it home and hide it. It was all agreed that we needed to go our separate ways and move out of Ireland.

November 26, 1795

I read no more of Joseph Allen Dyland's journal. My questions of the gold were answered and I was relieved to know that he was not a pirate and murderer. Although he acquired his fortune by not-so-honest means, maybe I would have done the same thing if I had been in his shoes. My consolation now that was setting my mind at ease was the fact that I was using it for charitable purposes. *So where was this old house going to lead me now?* I asked myself. *And were there any more secrets it was hiding in its shadows?*

I looked around in that cellar on the east end of the house and in it's great expanse amid more of the same ramblings of generations of Dylands. I could almost imagine from their leavings of parts of their lives and picture them and hear their voices from baby cries in their bassinets to young children playing with their toys. I saw christening gowns and little girl and boy's clothes. I saw them as they become young adults and their sport games they played. I saw the family, their picnic baskets, and their fishing gear. I saw them down at the lake, shouting as they pulled out large fish. I saw trunks full of beautiful gowns of satin and silk and wigs they wore to balls. I saw hats of the most elegant ribbons and feathers and sequins and button top shoes. I saw books of the most intellect on science, law, banking, medicine, religion, and various other subjects of interest. I saw families well lived, and I felt like I was born too late. I could feel their presence and see myself among them engaging in all their family gatherings, and I felt a sense of belonging and peace with this family of Dylands.

I trod back up the cellar stairs with a different feeling than I had when I went down. It was a good one and I felt a feeling of relief come over me like a lifted cloud of fog. Now everything had more meaning to me and I had a renewed sense of this old house and its history and beauty.

—�ᵚ—

Frank was doing better with his phobia and was able to get a part-time job in the city. He still liked to do the yard work here and he did a great job. He was someone around to help with other things that came up. He had more self-esteem and was becoming more and more confident in himself and being around others. It was heartwarming to see the results of my therapy working.

CHAPTER 20

The years were creeping up on me, and at this stage in my life, I tried to cram in all the living I could. I still was seeing Tom when I went to Paris. Each time I saw him, I still tasted that sweet chocolate. I think I wanted to share all my life with him and tell him just how much I loved him, regardless of our arrangement. I didn't care that he may have been married or he may be a criminal.

I was set to go to Paris the next day and was rehearsing how I would tell him how I felt and to tell him that I wanted to share everything about my life with him. I was hoping that he would want to share his life with me, too, and was hoping that part of it would be that he was not married. I wanted to bring him home with me and show him my beautiful mansion. I wanted to tell him everything about my family, my Mum, and Maggie. I wanted to tell him about the gold and my forefathers. The secrets in me were bursting to come out and be told. I had kept them long enough. I felt confident enough that I could trust him in all things. I just couldn't wait to see him again.

I slept soundly that night, but with a dream similar to the one I had before of dancing with a familiar looking man. I could feel the warmth of his body and see the glow of his eyes, and I know now that he resembled my grandfather, Joseph Allen Dylan, whose picture hung in the front foyer. We were dancing again to the same tune, his song, and he was saying to me in French, "*Chaque individu doit affronter son propre esprit et conscience et peu sont prêts à braver la désapprobation et la colère de la soci été.*" I couldn't understand it at first, but when I woke, the words were still in my head. I kept going over and over them and knowing fairly good French, I figured them out.

"*Every individual must confront his own mind and conscience, and few are willing to brave the disapproval and wrath of society.*" Could I judge my forefathers and their sins? I think not. "So where do I go from here?" I asked myself. Would I have any more dreams of Grandfather Joseph Allen or was his spirit now at rest in this house? Would there be any more spirits that aren't?

I boarded the train again the next morning. As I was riding on the just under three hour trip, I ran through my mind the dream of last night. What exactly are dreams? Can dreams guide you on your journey through life, can they warn you of certain dangers, and can they reveal certain information? The mystery of dreams has never been scientifically proven out as to how they have a connection to the subconscious mind. I know some dreams are so jumbled up that they don't make sense and are so farfetched they are beyond silly. I know my dreams of Joseph Allen have been an accumulation of mystery and information and have guided me by his spirit, which I think will always live in his house, but I feel at ease with them now.

—⁓—

Do you really want me to tell you something really subversive? Love is everything it's cracked up to be. It really is worth fighting for, being brave for, risking everything for. —Erica Jong

The train was slowing down and my heart began to race at the thought of seeing Tom again. He was the light of my life and the beat of my heart. His gentle spirit enveloped my whole being. Peering out the train window, I saw him, as usual, waiting for the train to stop. I loved everything about him, the way he walked, his voice, his neatness of dress, his finely combed hair, and trimmed mustache, and wondered how I could be so lucky to love and be loved by this wonderful man.

Tom met me with open arms and I just melted in his arms. I didn't realize that I had missed him so much. We decided to try a different restaurant this time for lunch, so we went to the Café de Paris. The restauranteur, Mr. Boubier, was famous for his original butter with which he added multiple spices, herbs, and other ingredients and served on cuts of choice beef. People of all localities sought it out for its mouthwatering goodness. We settled in the coziness of a corner table and ordered cocktails and, of course, we had to try his specialty. The warm nectar of the butter hit our palates like a scrumptious sensation on our tongues and the beef so tender rendered the most satisfaction of taste. We ended the most delectable meal with several cocktails that turned our mood into a calm and dreamy state of mind that made us want to cling together our warm bodies as lovers venture into that world of sensuality.

We made our way to the hotel and got the same room as always. I was still amazed at the beauty of the Hotel Le Bristol and the fresh flowers so fragrant always took my breath away as Tom picked a gardenia and placed it in my hair. We were like, as always, young married couples on their honeymoon. As we entered the room, my eyes widened as it was filled from wall to wall with flowers. There was a card from Tom to me with a simple line "Will you marry me?" My heart turned to mush and I had to sit down. I did not expect that and I could not say "no." As he knelt down, he placed the most beautiful diamond on my finger and his arms went around me and the chocolate flavor was the most intense I had ever tasted. His lips found mine and we sought each other's bodies out with the hot desires of young teenagers.

—∽—

*What is wanted is not the will to believe, but the will
to find out, which is the exact opposite.*
—Bertrand Russell

There were lots of things to talk about and to plan for. We knew each other, but we didn't know each other. One question was answered, we both weren't married, which was one of the most feared one for me. He didn't know that I was the richest woman in the world, but no one else knew either. I still had to make the decision whether to tell him or not. What about him and his financial condition? I didn't even know what his career was. Did he have any children? I never asked about his family—and I had agreed to marry this man. We both had stuck by our "no-ask" policy from the very beginning, but now was the time to begin asking questions, and lots of them, but I knew nothing could spoil the love I had for Tom.

The next morning we went about our routine as usual and I glanced down at my finger as the sun glinted on the diamond of the ring. *What was I thinking?* I asked myself. The fresh cool air of the morning hit my face and I became totally alert. Was it the wine, the coziness and ambiance of the restaurant, the room full of flowers and the mood of Paris that I got caught up in? How could I have said "yes" to marriage? The thought of the night before was like a fairy-tale dream in which I was the princess and Tom was the prince. What was I going to do about it?

The president of the bank greeted me as usual, and I made the exchange and deposit to the foundation's account. This trip definitely was not like my usual trip, and I felt a tremendous pressure that gave me an eerie feeling in the pit of my stomach that I almost felt nauseous. Tom and I had departed with an understanding that I would call him when I arrived back home.

The train ride back home was almost like a blur. I didn't notice the beautiful landscapes and all the other sights that I always enjoyed on my trips. All my mind was on was Tom and my acceptance of his ring. Looking down on its loveliness, I slipped it off and wrapped it in my handkerchief and placed it in a pocket of my handbag. Why did he do that? Everything was fine like it was. I loved Tom, but I still knew very little about him and his life. I knew, in a vulnerable moment, that I wanted to share everything with him, but reality and caution came to the fact that I had to be so very careful. Rosehaven couldn't be the only thing that had secrets, and I felt maybe he did. He was just too perfect.

I called him when I arrived back home and tried not to let him know what I had been thinking and I don't think he suspected anything. I had already decided to return his ring on my next trip and to tell him that I needed more time. In the meantime, I was going to hire a private detective to check into his life and to find out just what he was all about. After all, I was a rich widow, all alone, and just ripe for the picking, or was I?

I discovered a Mr. Jonas Allen deemed to be one of the most sought-after private detectives in Paris. We met for the initial interview and he agreed to look into my case and get started on it in the next couple of days. I never thought I would need a detective for anything, but life always brings changes and not all of them are good. I just wanted to live my life without any problems brought on by my own accord.

I nestled in my favorite chair by the fire and tried not to think on the negative aspects of Tom. Maybe I was just being too cautious and paranoid about him. Maybe he was truly the wonderful man he seemed to be and I would get the report that he is just a regular, fine, and upstanding person I thought he was. If I got that kind of report, then I was going to feel ashamed that I doubted him in the first place. If I got a report that he was not, then I am glad that he didn't know where I live, or does he? I only told him that I lived in London. Just to be cautious, I had more security placed on the gates to Rosehaven. I told myself that I needn't worry about anyone knowing about the gold and treasure. How could anyone know? I had told no one. The only way anyone would know is when I deposited the gold bars at the bank. Maybe I should have held up awhile. I thought I should go to America and set up an account there.

When Tom called that night, I told him that my business in Paris had slacked off for a while and I wouldn't be returning for some time. He wanted to come to London to see me, but I told him I was going to America to visit a sick friend. My investigator needed the time to do his work and it was a good excuse not to see Tom. I didn't think I could face him just then, knowing I was suspicious of his intentions and that I had a detective looking into his background.

—⚹—

I booked my passage on the Queen Mary again to New York. It was strange traveling there again without my sister and traveling at my age alone. My age was creeping up on me and I felt like I wouldn't be able to make many more trips. Although I was still in good health, I didn't feel comfortable being in another country without a companion.

The Queen Mary ship had undergrown a lot of history since Mary and I made our virgin trip on it in 1939 to the New York World Fair. It was the biggest, fastest, and more powerful than its predecessor, the Titanic. It had been painted gray and turned into a warship to transport soldiers in the Second World War and renamed The Grey Ghost. It could accommodate as many as fifteen thousand men. It was outfitted with a degaussing coil that helped alter the ship's magnetic field and helped with the protection of the use of the enemy's magnetic mines. Many soldiers died on it and later it was deemed to be haunted. There were many ghost stories, and some say she is riddled with cold spots, phantom figures, and muffled voices. Room number 340 was haunted by sheets flying off their beds while people are in them and loud taps and bangs on the walls. The pool area was said to have lovely ladies with swim suits of the 1930s laughing and leaving their wet foot-prints. A little girl named "Jackie" that drowned was said to walk around the pool clutching her teddy bear. Another tale was that a tall man was said to walk the corridors smiling. In room B-74, a father murdered his wife and two daughters and killed himself. It was said that one daughter named Dana liked the archive and cargo area and called out to her mother near the second-class pool area. It was said that a man with a beard and wearing blue work overalls wanders the shaft alley before disappearing around Door number 13. After the war, it took ten months to be retrofitted before it could go back into commercial passenger service. It had added more berths in all three classes and air conditioning. She resumed her voyages in July 1947.

I am not a believer in the paranormal, but I believe some spirits are not fully at rest. I have had patients who swore that they could see ghosts. Many of them were ghosts of the people they had wronged and it's their conscience at work. Who knows, I thought then, maybe I will see some on this trip and I would change my mind. Anyway, I was looking forward to seeing New York again.

The cool ocean breeze hit my face as I looked out over the rippled water. A flock of seagulls flew by and their whiteness filled the blue sky like snow. The ship seemed to be only half-filled with passengers, and I felt so thankful that I could experience these glories of God's uniqueness and man's indulgence of grandeur. I never saw any of the ghosts. Maybe I would see one on my return trip.

—⟋⟍—

New York had definitely changed, and, of course, all the ado about the fair was gone. I settled into my hotel room and got a bite to eat in the hotel restaurant. It was afternoon by then and the hotel was within walking distance of the bank. I had made an appointment with the top manager to set up an account for the foundation.

With my business finished, I wandered the busy streets and did some shopping. That night I went to the theater for a Broadway show. *Hello Dolly* was playing, and I had forgotten how much I loved New York and all its glamour and entertainment, but it was not the same without Mary. I missed her so much at times that I thought I would not be able to stand it and had to shake myself to reality. Why would a god of love take away all my loved ones from me? It was not fair. Then I would think of Tom, I felt I truly loved him. But was his love for me true? I would soon find out.

I arrived back in South Hampton the next evening and drove back to Rosehaven. Frank had some of his famous soup made and I had a bowl full and conked out. I was thankful for him taking care of everything around the place. He seemed to have only a few bouts of his phobia, and they didn't last very long. When he felt one coming, he just went outside, took in the fresh air, and tuned his mind to something nice in his life.

The next day I went to the shelter to see if everything was running smoothly. I was again thankful that I had good people to work there. Some were volunteers and were deeply dedicated to helping with the homeless. The old man who knew Mum Maggie as a young girl on the streets, asked about her. I had to tell him that she had died. I didn't understand before when he saw Maggie that he had known her as a streeter and she had pretended not to know him for she knew he would give her secret away. Everything comes out in the end.

The next day I helped Frank around in the yard. We had to prepare the beds for springtime if we were going to have the lavish display of flowers we always had. Our roses were the most beautiful and none could compare to them. Photographers from magazines were always asking to photograph them and some of the brides around London wanted to have their marriage photos taken by them and the house. I am very thankful that I have been able to enjoy such beauty in my own surroundings. The many varieties of flowers and shrubs with their many colors looked like a fairy tale wonderland and their scents rivaled the most expensive perfume.

It had been almost three weeks and I hadn't gotten an update on Tom. I was informed from the beginning that it would take a good while. Nevertheless, I was getting impatient without knowing one way or the other. Tom had called and I had to put him off with saying I had some things here to take care of. I hoped he couldn't hear anything different in my voice to get suspicious, although it was getting harder and harder. Being the kind of person I am, I hated to mislead anyone about anything, and I felt a few pangs of guilt. What if this private detective thing was for naught and I would feel like a distrustful person? Anyway, I brushed the hair from my face and went back into the house for a cool glass of tea.

Doubts began to cloud my mind and I couldn't sleep that night. There's no way anyone knew about the gold except the bank and I only took a few bars at time for deposit. They knew I had inherited the mansion and probably thought that they just came from Mr. Dyland's private collection. Money matters of the bank's clients are supposed to be confidential just like lawyers and doctors code of ethics. How could Tom know about the fortune I had in my possession and, for the most part, anything else about my finances? I began to get that guilt feeling about hiring a private detective again. How could I doubt the man who had become so dear to my heart?

The next day I busied myself about the house and not getting too far from the telephone. I had warned detective Allen about our phone system. It was in the years of party lines where you shared the lines with others. Each party or household would have a certain number of rings for their calls but sometimes some would pick up on another's ring and listen in. He was only to give me non-confidential information like maybe a place to meet me or a time convenient for him to come to the house. Mine was two short rings. About two o'clock that afternoon, my phone rang those two short rings and it was the detective. He was to come to my house that evening to discuss what he had found.

My heart was racing and I had to sit down to catch my breath. They say curiosity killed the cat and it was about to kill me. I readied myself and sat on the porch to get some fresh air and waited till almost time for him to arrive. My kitty took the opportunity to get some petting as she jumped into my lap and the sound of her soft purring calmed me and the anticipation of not hearing good news vanished from my mind.

It seemed like hours before I heard the entry alarm at the gate. My heart was beating overtime as I let the detective through the door. He walked with a cane and carried with him a black leather case. As we sat down in the library, I offered tea and cakes. We made all the small talk about Rosehaven as he drank the hot tea and devoured the small cakes. He seemed in no hurry to get down to business, but I was shaking and feeling like I was having a hot flash coming on and a migraine. As he stuffed the last cake down and drank a second cup of tea, he sat the briefcase on the coffee table, punched in the code, unsnapped the lock, lifted the lid, and pulled out a handful of papers and photos. "As I have said before, I have had cases like this before."

Detective Allen said. "I knew this case was probably linked to the others, and it should be exposed to the proper authorities. First, I have to be certain that I am investigating the same man you have hired me to investigate. Is this the photo of your Tom?" He asked as he held a full-page photo up.

I couldn't give him Tom's last name, because he didn't give it to me, and I didn't give him mine but I had a picture of us together taken in Paris at one of those self-portrait booths.

"Absolutely," I replied.

His handsome face starred back at me and I had the worst feeling of guilt, but I didn't know what I was about to discover and I was completely unprepared.

Detective Allen laid the photo to one side and picked up a single page out of the thick stack.

"Now, I have had to deal with situations like this before and I want you to try and not get upset. Just realize that I am here to help you and I have your best interest at heart. This Tom is an alias name. His real name is Michael McClinton, and he doesn't live in Paris, he lives in London. He has used other aliases, John Jones, Josh Freeman, Norman Williams, Fred Johnson, should I go on?"

My heart fell and I put my hands over my face and lowered my head. The terrible dismay I felt rendered me speechless and I ran into the kitchen for a few moments to compose myself. How could someone do this? And how could I be so blind to let it happen?

I splashed cold water on my face and returned back to the library. Detective Allen was waiting patiently and asked if I was alright and if I needed more time before he went on. I nodded that he could continue. He picked up eight full-page photos with this Michael, each with a different woman. I knew he had to have had a past with different women.

"These weren't just women, these were very rich women he supposedly married and never divorced any of them," he said.

He wiggled his way into all their lives, schemed, and took all their money. You are just lucky and smart enough that you found out before he could do his dirty work. *His dirty work*, I said to myself, is breaking a heart dirty enough? I did feel a sense of realization that one more of these secrets of life were revealed. And I wondered how many more secrets I would have to solve.

"You know, Ms. Anna, not many know of what this man was involved in. This Tom belonged to an organization of gigolos. The name of it is The Morris Company and it supposedly sells fitness machinery. They work in twos, where one man investigates the woman's finances to make sure that she is loaded, single, lonely, and looking for a man. He stalks her without her knowing him and learns all her habits, comings, and goings. Then all the investigators meet with the gigolos and make their plans. They are very well organized and worth millions.

I couldn't believe what he was telling me. I knew there were pimps for prostitution of women, but not an organization for men to take such advantages of them by taking their money. How could Tom and his investigator know about me? I had been so careful. They couldn't have known about the gold. I had told no one. I asked Detective Allen how did this happen to me, and he said it was probably because I lived in this mansion and owned so much land and I went to the bank so often. Could Tom have gone through my luggage each time we were together when I was sleeping and found the gold bars? That must have been a great big bonus for him. It seems to make sense now, I wasn't as careful as I thought because I trusted him.

Detective Allen knew I needed to be alone to think things out. He said he was sorry to be the bearer of bad news, but that I would be better off knowing just what kind of man this Tom was. I shook his hand, thanked him, and saw him out. Yes, I would have plenty of time to think about this situation. How was I going to break it off with this gigolo, that scoundrel that had stolen my heart while trying to steal my money? I thought about the ring he gave me. Was it even real? I would have liked to have shoved it up his ass and with my red-headed temper, I wasn't beyond doing it.

I didn't sleep at all that night. Tears of my broken heart left my pillow case damp as I left my bed early the next morning. I picked up my kitty as she brushed against my legs and hugged her close to me as I made my way to the kitchen, asking myself how I could be so stupid. I began to get angrier and angrier, but after a few minutes I calmed down and thanked my lucky stars that I found out before he set his final plan in place. The question now was: How was I going to break it off and get my revenge?

I went into the drawing room, kneeled on my prayer stool, and said a prayer, asking my savior for guidance in my life and to give thanks for my many blessings. I prayed for Tom and his coworkers that they may see the evil in their lives and repent. I prayed and thanked him for each day he had given me and to give me the strength to face my enemies and to forgive them.

I always felt better when I prayed. It gave me a sense of solace and a renewal of my senses just as it does whenever I walk in the green pastures and feel the sun and breeze on my face. It's as if I can hear the song birds singing and I can smell the sweet scent of the pine trees and the white and yellow honeysuckles. It's a new awakening of the peace in my mind and soul and gives me that warm feeling in my heart. Believe me; I needed to do a lot of praying.

For right then, I had to try to put it out of my mind and get on with my life. I felt very vulnerable now knowing that I had been watched and followed and was completely unaware of it. I would be more observant of my surroundings whenever I left the gates of Rosehaven from then on out.

—⁂—

The days and nights passed by and my mind was in a fog. I felt completely out of it and just trying to get out of bed was a struggle. I knew I had to pull myself together because I was beginning to get in a deep depression. I had no one; everyone had left me, now Tom or whoever he was at that moment in time was gone from me, too. I was a trained physiatrist and I knew what was happening to me. Even doctors get sick, but I knew what I had to do. I had to pull myself together and get my rump out of that bed and out of that house.

I went back to New York, and this time, I rented a flat for six months. I brought enough of the gold bars to deposit a few at a time. My money allowed me to go anywhere I wanted to go. I enjoyed the Broadway shows, shopping, and sight-seeing, and I met some wonderful people who became good friends. It was just what I needed to help heal my wounded heart and forget the sad times in my life. I had even planned a trip to the tropics for the wintertime. Maybe I could be a beach bum and get tanned like the locals.

—ന—

It had been a year since I had sailed the Queen Mary back to New York. I had begun to miss Rosehaven and the vastness of the land. Frank had done a great job holding the fort down. The yard looked spectacular with all the roses blooming. Everything looked so immaculate. I was hoping with time gone by, the business with Tom and his cronies would have disappeared. I had sent that cheap ring to the Morris Company with attention to Michael McClinton, and I hope he got the message. There were no messages or letters to me from him when I got home and that was a good thing.

So it seemed that another phase in my life had come and gone. Life is full of joys, disappointments, failures, and, most of all, surprises. Some of the happenings in our lives would never be so conceivable to have even been thought of, yet here they have been. I never would have thought that my life could have been so magical and awesome yet so disconcerted.

CHAPTER 21

It had been a long time since I had been to the soup kitchen, and while I was gone, I had drawn up plans to have everything remodeled and that new addition built on it. I even missed that good soup they made and was anxious to get there, see everybody, and discuss everything I had in mind to do. Some of the regulars were there, and it was nice to see them again. I needed to be around people whom I loved and who loved me.

I busied myself with the construction of the new soup kitchen remodel, and after a month, it was finished and filled to capacity. I was still thankful for the faithful people I had working, and it didn't require much of my time. I still had the second cellar to finish cleaning out and was hopeful that I would find some more good stuff to donate.

The world was changing so much in everything as it was 1980 and my life, now at seventy, seemed to be flying away like the leaves in the wind at autumn. How quickly the years go by! I wondered what my future would bring.

After all these years of living at Rosehaven, it still amazed me, and I was still finding things I had never seen before. The family Bible was the most valuable part of the history of this old house. The scrap books told stories of the inhabitants with photos and newspaper clippings. It was my greatest pleasure each night to settle in the library with a cup of hot tea and browse through them and the old books. I tried to match up all the family in order of birth and which children belonged to whom. As far as I could tell, all were buried in the family cemetery, but there was one daughter's tombstone missing and I wondered where she might be buried.

Mornings were the time of day that I liked to get started in the cellar. I took my light down the dark stairway to the musky bottom. I did find a light switch and it illuminated most of the vast darkness. Although my forefathers had kept the house in almost perfect order, that cellar was piled with stuff on top of each other and I had a hard time making a path to get through. Everything I saw was of the most high-end quality and I didn't question how, because I knew. They had lived in complete luxury from the first patriarch till my grandfather. I still don't believe that my grandfather knew about the treasure. I believed he had acquired his wealth on his own, otherwise why didn't he find some way for me to know?

I looked through and sorted a pile of things for the yard sale. They could use some things in the new addition of the soup kitchen and called it a day. I got Frank to come down and bring it all up. My age was beginning to get the best of me. I had a bite to eat and drifted off to sleep on the sofa. I was awakened by the ringing of the phone, but I was too groggy to answer it. Suddenly, I became fully alert when I heard a familiar voice on the answer machine. It was Tom or whoever he called himself. How dare he call? The scoundrel! I was never going to talk to him, and if he continues to call, I'd have my number changed and that would be the end of that. I managed to get up and get a shower and fell right to sleep.

The next day I resumed my plundering in the cellar and got quite a lot of stuff to be donated. While it was exhausting going through the dusty cobwebs, I found it quite fun and I was continuously looking for clues to my heritage. I had always heard that these old houses had hidden rooms and although I had already found one, I knew there were probably more. Where there were built in shelves, I was always knocking on them or looking for some kind of a button to push and see if they would miraculously open.

After going through stacks of boxes, I came across one marked JOHN WESLEY DYLAND. It contained quite a number of books, papers, and memorabilia. He was the second generation to reside in the house and also his daughter, Cecelia Rose, was the one who was missing in the cemetery. Accordingly to the family Bible, she was born in 1819 and died in 1837 at only 18 years old. I eagerly went through everything in the wooden box and then I found a number of journals from members of his family. What a trove of treasures I had found! These would give me lots of information about what kind of lives they had led. Actually there was one from Cecelia herself. Since she had died so young, I was anxious to learn the cause of her death. I moved several more books and found her father's journal.

I didn't know which one to start reading first. They were both amazingly well preserved in the sealed wooden box. John Paul's was, of course, leather bound and well worn, but Cecelia's was very feminine and bound together with pink ribbons and covered with French lace now yellowed with age. A semblance of a bouquet of red roses graced the front cover. I had my reading material for the evening as I managed to climb the stairs back to the library. I couldn't wait to get started.

Another day had passed and I had forgotten about the phone call Mr. Tom had made earlier. They say there is a small, thin line between love and hate and what's that about a woman scorned? I was determined to try to put all of that out of my mind and concentrate on the family I had and the family I could have had.

Mable had been at the house, cleaning all day. She had prepared a nice dinner for me, and I was ready to crash and eat. After a short nap, I was ready to settle down and start reading the journals. My kitty snuggled against me for some petting. She always made me feel calm as her soft purring vibrated against my neck.

The choice of which one to start on first was quite a challenge. I was wondering what kind of a man John Paul was, but my curiosity as to why Cecelia Rose died so early won out. I opened the front cover of her journal and thought that I smelled a faint scent of perfume, maybe rosemary or cloves. It seems she didn't start her journal till she was twelve. It was filled with small drawn hearts and stars and just the little preteen musings about growing up and all about her first boyfriend and her first kiss. I skipped on over toward the end and she was telling about the new horse her daddy had bought for her and how she couldn't wait to ride him. That was the last entry in her journal. *What could have happened to her?* I wondered. Did the horse throw her and kill her? Or did she get sick from some disease and just died? Maybe she just didn't want to write anything anymore. No, I looked at the last entry date. It was the day before she died. Now my curiosity was really working overtime and I couldn't wait to go to the same date on her father's journal.

I felt a real connection to Cecelia, but yet sorrow for such a young woman. Her dying at such a young age and thinking of her not growing up to be a bride and mother and experiencing all that life would have offered her, brought tears to my eyes. I had to take a few minutes to compose myself before I opened the brown, worn leather journal of her father.

I could smell the muskiness and leather and maybe a hint of cigar smoke as I unwound the string that held the journal closed. Several photos fell out onto my lap and I quickly grasped them before they fell onto the dusty floor of the cellar. One was a photo of a lady probably in her early twenties. She was beautiful with hair atop her head and a low cut smocked bodice revealing full breasts and wearing a pearl necklace and matching earrings. The second was a photo of a younger woman, perhaps in her middle teens and just as beautiful wearing the same style dress with her hair down in long flowing curls. I was certain these were the photos of his wife, Elsa, and his daughter, Cecelia.

John Wesley Dyland's journal ended in 1837. I thumbed through the thick pages to the date of Cecelia's death. The pages were smeared and difficult to read. I believed they had gotten wet with tears as he made an account of that horrendous day. It started as follows:

Today has been the worst day of my life, and I write this with a broken heart as I have lost my beautiful and dear daughter Cecelia Rose. The end of her life has come too soon and she has risen to her father in heaven to be held in his arms for all eternity. I cannot describe the sadness I feel at the loss of her wonderful spirit. She was my only daughter and the love of everyone she came in contact with. I could deny there is a God for why would he take my reason for living, my angel, to be one of his? I have been raised to love the Lord, but how could I do that now? He took my beloved wife, Elsa, in childbirth but gave me Cecelia, but thank God I still have a son, John Paul.

I skimmed through more pages of John Wesley's journal, but how Cecelia died was never mentioned. I thought that was very odd. Maybe he couldn't bear to write it and gaze upon the written words of her early demise. I would have to look elsewhere to find that out.

It was still early afternoon when I decided to give up sorting in the cellar. I hadn't had lunch, so I settled for a cold sandwich and a glass of red wine. A starling was outside of the window and his shrill call echoed through the veranda. Why hadn't I noticed the birds out here before? Was it because I had been so caught up with the gold, Tom, and this old mansion? I vowed to myself to chill out and enjoy the beauty all around me as I breathed in the scent of the gardenia bouquet by my table.

As the day wore on, I could not get Cecelia out of my mind, even though I had tried to think of other things. She was a beautiful young woman, and she had her whole life before her. I knew what her father went through for I had gone through it, too, by losing Manning and then losing Johann. Life doesn't seem fair sometimes when we lose our loved ones to death, no matter how or when it comes.

—⟋⟍⟋—

I slept fitfully that night with old dreams coming back and not making any sense at all. My kitty stirred underneath the blankets. I feared she would smother to death, but she always rooted herself out as she leaped down to hunt for her litter box and food. I had planned to get back down the cellar to resume my quest for the cause of Cecelia's death, in fact I couldn't wait. I plugged the coffee pot in and flopped two pieces of bread in the toaster, opened the refrigerator for some of Mable's plum jam and began to start my day.

John Wesley's journal laid there just as I had left it, and as I looked at it, I wondered if it was going to contain any answers to my questions and any more information about the rest of my bygone family. I still felt like I had been born too late and I should have a journal lying around here, too, wrapped in ribbons and smelling like potpourri or maybe a hint of gardenia. *What would have been my story of those long ago years?* I wondered.

I picked up the journal and skimmed through the pages beyond Cecelia's death date, still no mention. Why? I wondered. Maybe that page had been torn out, but I saw no evidence of any page missing or being torn from the binding. I skimmed through about twenty more of the written pages and then something caught my eye. There was a folded piece of paper like some kind of invoice. It was from a company that made cast-iron caskets. I looked at the date and was sure enough that it was dated one week after Cecelia's death. The amount seemed to be quite a lot for a casket especially in that time.

I read farther and was about to find out some very astonishing information that I wasn't prepared for. It was dated September 26, 1837:

I visited my beautiful daughter today. I finally got myself composed enough to see her. [*What did he mean, see her? Did he visit her grave?* I asked myself for she died on June 9) She was just as beautiful as always. She still had that winning smile that drew everyone to her. She looked like she was just sleeping and waiting for her prince charming to kiss her and wake her.

That seemed too weird to me, and I thought maybe he had had an emotional breakdown.

I read farther:

It's so heartbreaking for me to write about the death of my only daughter, but I feel like it might bring me a little closure by putting it down on paper. Cecelia died instantly from a clot in her brain. I couldn't bring myself to put her in a dark grave where I would never see her sweet face again, so I purchased a cast-iron casket that has a glass top. They have a method of preserving the body by some sort of sealing process keeping all air out. The body will be perpetually preserved as long as the seal is not ever broken, and if it gets broken, the body will disintegrate. I have placed her at the end of the bunker in a secret room where she will be protected and remain beautiful forever. It was hard to enter the bunker room today for the first time to visit her, not knowing whether the process of burial would work, but there she was. I held my breath as I glanced upon her sweet face, just as perfect as the day she died. I laid a bouquet of the pink roses, her favorite, on the top of the glass. Now I could rest knowing I could come here and visit her anytime and tell her how much I loved and missed her.

Oh, gosh! That was a lot to take in, because I had never heard of such a thing. And I asked myself if I could take on the task of finding that secret room and worse still could I bear to cast my eyes on a woman who had been dead for so long? Could this be true that she would still be as young and beautiful as she was at the time of her burial? It seemed preposterous to me that such a thing would be possible, but the only way I could find out would be to find that secret room.

I thought and thought that night as I lay awake and wondered if I should search for that secret room. Maybe it wasn't meant for anyone to find, and maybe it would be bad luck for me if I did find it. Certainly, just like the gold, I couldn't tell anyone about it. Everybody would want to come to see her. If word got out, the media would spread it out everywhere, and my privacy at Rosehaven would be gone. Certainly, both of the secrets at Rosehaven would be hard to keep secret, but I had to do it.

I woke suddenly and rose up in my bed with an echo of something in my head, maybe from a dream or maybe the last ding of the telephone or chime from the grandfather clock in the hallway. I had a weird feeling that I was not alone, but I shrugged it off. The day before had left me with a feeling of uneasiness, and I couldn't shake it. I wanted to go down in the bunker that morning, but I couldn't bring myself to even make an attempt. With my nerves on edge, I decided I needed to get away from this old mansion. It had given me another secret that I wasn't prepared to deal with at that time.

I busied myself around with breakfast and dressing. Whenever I needed space, I always headed to the bluff above the river. I could never get enough of nature, and I wasn't disappointed that day because the honeysuckles were blooming and their sweet scent was like a sedative to my whole being. The mere touch of the soft breeze sent light and fresh caresses on my face and hair, and I breathed it in as if it was the finest of opium. The warn sun bathed my bare arms, and it felt like a loving hug from Mum. How I missed her and yet couldn't help thinking about her long-kept secret.

I stood there on the bluff, watching the ripples of the flowing water like rhinestones, sparkling their brilliance. The banks covered with patches of wild flowers of all shades of colors beckoned the tiny hummingbirds and butterflies to taste their sweet nectar. What a beautiful world God had created for everyone to enjoy, yet some barely took notice of it.

I returned back to the house, grabbed my purse and keys, and lit out for the city. Shopping for a new hat and outfit and going to the shops always made me feel better. First, I went to Mary's old shop and bought a new pair of shoes. Then I went across town to another popular shop and bought one of the latest style hats and a new dress. I don't know why I thought I needed something new. I had nowhere to wear them. I thought it was just a lady thing and great for relieving stress. After shopping, I popped in the soup kitchen for a cup of soup and to check in and then went back home.

—✺—

Frank was working on setting out some fruit trees. I had the thought that I would get him to go down in the bunker with me. It would make me feel better having someone with me when I found the secret room with the cast-iron coffin. Then it hit me just like it did when I felt like I would share the thing about the gold with Tom, but I sure am glad that I didn't. It would probably have been a major disaster. I couldn't. I would just have to go by myself and never breathe a word to anyone.

The next day was the big day and I was nervous. Armed with a good flashlight with extra batteries, I ventured down the long bunker. There were electric lights there, but I didn't want to take the chance of being at the end of it with no light. It was a good thing, too, that steps had been taken to keep it ventilated and the temperature was comfortable. I hadn't been down there since we all came there to be safe from the bombings during the war.

I had never been to the very end of the bunker, and I didn't realize that it was so long, but I carried on. Grandfather John Allen had to spend his money in some way, and I was glad that he had this bunker made. If we had been struck from air raids during the war, we wouldn't have survived, if not for that shelter. A secret room was spoken of in the diary, and I was wondering if I would be able to find it. I was hoping that it would not require a key or a code, because I had no idea where the key might be much less a code. If it did, I would have to go back in the cellar and that would be another search I would have to do. Maybe if it required a code, it would be written somewhere in his journal that I hadn't read yet, perhaps in the back.

I looked on ahead as I passed a wall with a light, but the far distance looked dark and I wondered why I didn't bring some extra light bulbs. Thank goodness, I brought a good flashlight, but it didn't help with the eeriness I felt. I wished I had brought Frank with me. Nevertheless, I was not about to quit now and my adrenaline was at its highest peak as I moved on to the end.

The massive framework of the bunker was right before me then, and I shined my light all around in search of a secret door. I saw nothing that even resembled a door, and I gave a sigh and wondered if my grandpa was in his right state of mind when he wrote that preposterous entry about a sealed coffin with a beautiful corpse that would always remain beautiful. I had never heard of such a thing. Shoot, every corpse decays. Well, then I thought, he did say it was a "secret" door, so I ran my hand over all the crevices of the walls. I was close to the end corner when suddenly the space under my hand began to move and I heard a squeaking noise. The wall opened wide to a doorway. My heart felt like it was about to jump out of my body and I couldn't help but move back and scream. I was immediately hit with the scent of dried roses and herbs. There stood the coffin, just as he had written. I slowly approached it, bracing myself for what I thought I might see. I slowly peeked over the edge of the glass enclosure and there she laid—Cecelia Rose, the most beautiful maiden I had ever seen. Her face was smooth and fair and she looked as if she was sleeping. Roses lay all around her. Her lips were pink and her hair cascaded around her shoulders in long curls. Her dress was white satin and trimmed with pink ribbons and lace. Her hands lay beside her. She clutched a white crocheted handbag with a blue handkerchief. She wore a pearl and diamond necklace around her neck and earrings of the same. It was hard to catch my breath as I peered upon her lovely face. I had to sit down in the chair beside her. That was so unreal to me. I felt like lifting the glass and waking her to hear her voice, for she didn't look like someone who had been dead for generations. I thought, *How could that be possible?* Yet here she was. I wondered how many times had her father visited her before his death. I knew this had to be a secret that had to remain secret, and I intended to see that it did.

Although this was my home and I loved it, things were getting just a little bit too weird. Maybe that's the way it is with old mansions as old as this one. Maybe, it is just me. I should find a smaller and newer place to live. The secret door closed behind me as I exited the tomb into the bunker hallway and made my way to the entrance. The light of the day hit my face and I breathed in the fresh air. How could I leave this beautiful place? No, I couldn't, just as my forefathers couldn't.

—⋘—

I thought I would pick some flowers and go and hug my kitty. That always helped whenever I was stressed out. What I had discovered that day certainly was something so unthinkable and amazingly remarkable. I sat on the sofa among all the pillows and drifted off to sleep.

When I awoke, it was early morning, and I thought of what had happened the day before. Had I dreamed all of that? But as I became fully awake, I realized that I hadn't. What other secrets this old house was willing to give up, I wondered and I hoped they would be happy ones.

—⋘—

For the next few weeks, Mable and I cleaned the house. The coal-burning fireplaces had been closed up and replaced with gas logs.